TESTING THE LIMITS: IRAN'S BALLISTIC MISSILE PROGRAM, SANCTIONS, AND THE ISLAMIC REVOLUTIONARY GUARD CORPS

HEARING

BEFORE THE

SUBCOMMITTEE ON
THE MIDDLE EAST AND NORTH AFRICA

OF THE

COMMITTEE ON FOREIGN AFFAIRS
HOUSE OF REPRESENTATIVES

ONE HUNDRED FIFTEENTH CONGRESS

FIRST SESSION

MARCH 29, 2017

Serial No. 115–14

Printed for the use of the Committee on Foreign Affairs

Available via the World Wide Web: http://www.foreignaffairs.house.gov/ or
http://www.gpo.gov/fdsys/

U.S. GOVERNMENT PUBLISHING OFFICE

24–834PDF   WASHINGTON : 2017

For sale by the Superintendent of Documents, U.S. Government Publishing Office
Internet: bookstore.gpo.gov   Phone: toll free (866) 512–1800; DC area (202) 512–1800
Fax: (202) 512–2104   Mail: Stop IDCC, Washington, DC 20402–0001

COMMITTEE ON FOREIGN AFFAIRS

EDWARD R. ROYCE, California, *Chairman*

CHRISTOPHER H. SMITH, New Jersey
ILEANA ROS-LEHTINEN, Florida
DANA ROHRABACHER, California
STEVE CHABOT, Ohio
JOE WILSON, South Carolina
MICHAEL T. McCAUL, Texas
TED POE, Texas
DARRELL E. ISSA, California
TOM MARINO, Pennsylvania
JEFF DUNCAN, South Carolina
MO BROOKS, Alabama
PAUL COOK, California
SCOTT PERRY, Pennsylvania
RON DeSANTIS, Florida
MARK MEADOWS, North Carolina
TED S. YOHO, Florida
ADAM KINZINGER, Illinois
LEE M. ZELDIN, New York
DANIEL M. DONOVAN, JR., New York
F. JAMES SENSENBRENNER, JR.,
    Wisconsin
ANN WAGNER, Missouri
BRIAN J. MAST, Florida
FRANCIS ROONEY, Florida
BRIAN K. FITZPATRICK, Pennsylvania
THOMAS A. GARRETT, JR., Virginia

ELIOT L. ENGEL, New York
BRAD SHERMAN, California
GREGORY W. MEEKS, New York
ALBIO SIRES, New Jersey
GERALD E. CONNOLLY, Virginia
THEODORE E. DEUTCH, Florida
KAREN BASS, California
WILLIAM R. KEATING, Massachusetts
DAVID N. CICILLINE, Rhode Island
AMI BERA, California
LOIS FRANKEL, Florida
TULSI GABBARD, Hawaii
JOAQUIN CASTRO, Texas
ROBIN L. KELLY, Illinois
BRENDAN F. BOYLE, Pennsylvania
DINA TITUS, Nevada
NORMA J. TORRES, California
BRADLEY SCOTT SCHNEIDER, Illinois
THOMAS R. SUOZZI, New York
ADRIANO ESPAILLAT, New York
TED LIEU, California

AMY PORTER, *Chief of Staff*   THOMAS SHEEHY, *Staff Director*

JASON STEINBAUM, *Democratic Staff Director*

———

SUBCOMMITTEE ON THE MIDDLE EAST AND NORTH AFRICA

ILEANA ROS-LEHTINEN, Florida, *Chairman*

STEVE CHABOT, Ohio
DARRELL E. ISSA, California
RON DeSANTIS, Florida
MARK MEADOWS, North Carolina
PAUL COOK, California
ADAM KINZINGER, Illinois
LEE M. ZELDIN, New York
DANIEL M. DONOVAN, JR., New York
ANN WAGNER, Missouri
BRIAN J. MAST, Florida
BRIAN K. FITZPATRICK, Pennsylvania

THEODORE E. DEUTCH, Florida
GERALD E. CONNOLLY, Virginia
DAVID N. CICILLINE, Rhode Island
LOIS FRANKEL, Florida
BRENDAN F. BOYLE, Pennsylvania
TULSI GABBARD, Hawaii
BRADLEY SCOTT SCHNEIDER, Illinois
THOMAS R. SUOZZI, New York
TED LIEU, California

CONTENTS

TESTING THE LIMITS: IRAN'S BALLISTIC MISSILE PROGRAM, SANCTIONS, AND THE ISLAMIC REVOLUTIONARY GUARD CORPS

WEDNESDAY, MARCH 29, 2017

House of Representatives,
Subcommittee on the Middle East and North Africa,
Committee on Foreign Affairs,
Washington, DC.

The subcommittee met, pursuant to notice, at 2:05 p.m., in room 2172, Rayburn House Office Building, Hon. Ileana Ros-Lehtinen (chairman of the subcommittee) presiding.

Ms. Ros-Lehtinen. The subcommittee will come to order. After recognizing myself and Ranking Member Deutch for 5 minutes each for our opening statements, I will then recognize other members seeking recognition for 1 minute or longer. We will then hear from our witnesses.

Without objection, witnesses, your prepared statements will be made a part of the record. Members may have 5 days in which to insert statements and questions for the record subject to the length limitation in the rules.

The Chair now recognizes herself for 5 minutes.

In the nearly 2 years since the United Nations Security Council adopted Resolution 2231, approving the Joint Comprehensive Plan of Action, JCPOA, and lifting sanctions on Iran, one thing has been abundantly clear: The notion that Iran would now modify its behavior and become a responsible member of the international community has proven to be completely and utterly false.

Many of us knew that the Iranian regime would not moderate its behavior, but that it would amplify its illicit activity using the nuclear deal as leverage. Sure enough, since the JCPOA was signed, we have seen an Iran that has taken U.S. citizens hostages and demanded, and unfortunately, received ransom for their return. As a result, Iran has since held additional U.S. citizens and permanent U.S. residents with the expectation of receiving more ransom payments.

The regime continues to support the Assad regime with money, supplies, weapons, fighters, and is doing the same in Yemen with the Houthis. Iran's ships have made dozens of provocative actions toward U.S. ships in the Strait of Hormuz and the Persian Gulf, with the regime playing a dangerous game and harassing our vessels.

Iran continues to support terror around the world, most notably through its support of the terror group Hezbollah. This has allowed Hezbollah to increase its stockpiled rockets and missiles to 150,000 or more and add more sophisticated missiles to its arsenal, putting our friend and ally, the democratic Jewish state of Israel, under greater threat.

All of these activities have seen an uptick since the JCPOA and all are indeed very troubling, but perhaps the most egregious and troubling is Iran's continued pursuit of a viable ballistic missile program. Why? Because history has shown us, and as one witness before this panel previously stated, that nuclear weapons and ballistic missile programs go hand in glove.

Over time, the correlation between a country's nuclear program and a corresponding ballistic missile program has proved to be absolute: That countries that sustain indigenous medium and long-range ballistic missiles always aspire to possess nuclear weapons.

Since the signing of the JCPOA, Iran has tested, according to some sources, at least 15 ballistic missiles, and it has done so in open defiance of Resolution 2231.

It came as a shock to so many of us that a final concession to Iran was given when the U.S. agreed to lift the arms embargo as part of the nuclear deal, especially when we were told repeatedly that the deal was only on the nuclear program. That is why the Trump administration needs to follow through on some of its promises and reevaluate the JCPOA and the 2231 resolution.

We are seeing an uptick in these ballistic missile tests and Iran's aspiration for an ICBM program, precisely because the regime wants to be ready to be able to deliver a nuclear payload when the terms of the JCPOA expire and we will have walked them right into it.

We simply cannot allow the regime to continue with these provocations. We need to go back to the Security Council and find a way to make sure that there can be no ambiguity. Any ballistic missile testing, any attempt to acquire ballistic missile technology or expertise, and any attempt to proliferate from the regime must be stopped and sanctioned.

The original intent of the nuclear sanctions was to put so much pressure on the regime that it would be forced to end all enrichment and completely dismantle its nuclear program and infrastructure. That needs to be our approach on the regime's missile program, while also revisiting the JCPOA and all of its flaws.

We already have important tools for the President to use now, like the Iran, North Korea, and Syria Nonproliferation Act. Sadly as this subcommittee learned last Congress, the State Department and the previous administration sat on these important reports and sanctions, oftentimes for years, in order to not upset the regime during these sensitive negotiations. The latest round of sanctions, on March 21, is a good step, but this report came 9 months after the previous report and only covered activities that took place in the year 2014. So we still have a very serious backlog.

The new administration needs to step up its Iran, North Korea, and Syria nonproliferation activities and it needs to use the other tools available to it. One tool should be Chairman Royce and Ranking Member Engel's new bill, of which I am proud to be a cosponsor, that specifically targets Iran's ballistic missiles.

We need Iran and those that seek to supply it with the technology or know-how to know that we will bring down sanctions so crippling on them that they will have to think twice about developing its ballistic missile program. We need to fully and vigorously enforce our current sanctions and then strengthen and expand them to ensure maximum pressure is exerted because Iran only responds to strength and pressure.

With that, I am pleased to yield to the ranking member, Mr. Deutch, for his opening statement.

Mr. DEUTCH. Thank you, Madam Chairman. Thanks for calling today's very timely hearing.

Iran is not a new subject for the subcommittee. We have explored its nuclear program, the threat it poses to Israel, its relationships with North Korea and Hezbollah, and the realities that it hopes to exploit under the JCPOA.

Today we will focus on Iran's nonnuclear behavior, its ballistic missile program and its dangerous Revolutionary Guard Corps. I know that you and I share the belief that this Congress can still move resolutely against Iran's continued pursuit of ballistic missiles. I want to thank our witnesses for being here to answer our questions and help us frame our conversation, and I look forward to what I know will be a healthy exchanges of ideas.

Despite the nuclear deal, Iran's behavior has not changed. Now freed from many of the sanctions that once isolated it, Iran is looking to integrate itself into the global economy and to normalize its relations with the Western countries. Unsurprisingly, this hope has been undermined by Iran's continued support for the murderous Assad regime in Syria, funding of Hezbollah in Lebanon, calls for the destruction of Israel, and insistence on sowing instability beyond its borders.

In many areas of conventional military power, Iran lags far behind its neighbors. To make up for these deficiencies, Iran now has the Middle East's largest arsenal of ballistic missiles and is developing the know-how to produce increasingly complex missile components on its own. Thanks to the Russians, Iran now has the S-300 missile defense system. And in a matter of a few years, the Iranian space program claims it will be able to create rockets that can drop a warhead anywhere in the world.

It is clear that left unhindered, the scale and the sophistication of the Iranian missile program will only grow, and it is incumbent on this Congress to act decisively to halt its progress. However Members may have felt about the nuclear deal, we can all agree that the JCPOA does not prevent us from responding to reckless behavior from Iran and that U.N. Security Council Resolution 2231 forbids the Iranians from testing or developing ballistic missiles.

Despite that resolution, the Iranian Revolutionary Guard Corps, which oversees the missile program, has conducted test after test of these weapons in defiance of the will of the international community. The fact that an organization like the IRGC, which supports terrorist organizations like Hamas and Hezbollah, is also in charge of dangerous missile technologies should send a chill down

4

the spine of anyone working for peace and stability in the Middle East.

The United States has an obligation to stand against the IRGC's repeated provocations by raising the issue of missile tests in the Security Council at every opportunity. We also need to use our influence at the U.N. to encourage allies to do the same, even at a time when our new President seems intent on abdicating America's role as a leader in international diplomacy.

In addition to robust engagement at the Security Council, we can take a number of concrete steps to box in the Iranians.

First, we need to pass the bipartisan H.R. 1698, which I am proud to cosponsor. The bill would sanction countries like Russia that sell missile technology to Iran, the financial institutions that make those sales possible, and the Iranian entities that contribute to the country's domestic missile industry.

Second, we have to support full and vigorous enforcement of the JCPOA, which means ensuring that the IAEA has the resources that it needs to carry out its monitoring, and, importantly, embracing Europe's renewed interest in tightening implementation of the deal.

Finally, we should encourage GCC states to adopt a coordinated missile defense system that will act as a deterrent to Iranian aggression in the Gulf.

I don't pretend that this list is exhaustive, and I am glad we have the opportunity today to discuss all of our options. Whatever path we take, it is clear that we must act together and that we must act quickly. The danger that Iran continues to pose through its funding of terrorist organizations, its meddling in regional affairs, and its pursuit of ever more deadly ballistic technologies demands continued engagement from the United States and our allies.

We have seen that international coordination against the threat from Iran is possible, and we know that there is strong bipartisan support in Congress for decisive action of this kind. I welcome a thoughtful discussion today about the tools we have at our disposal, and I encourage my colleagues to remain united against Iran's violations of international law and its clear refusal to live in peace with its neighbors.

And I will yield back the balance of my time. Thank you, Madam Chairman.

Ms. ROS-LEHTINEN. Thank you very much, Mr. Deutch.

And now we will turn to our members for their opening statements, starting with Mr. DeSantis of Florida.

Mr. DESANTIS. Thank you, Madam Chairman.

We have been on this committee years talking about Iran, talking about the Iran deal. We were told at the time this deal would help bring Iran into the community of nations, it would improve their behavior if we just let our boot off their neck and released all these sanctions. That hasn't happened here. We are talking about now their belligerence, what they are doing with ballistic missiles.

Go back to this deal. The Obama administration conceded at the outset on the ballistic missile issue, which was a major mistake to begin with. We see Iran has been emboldened by this deal, their belligerent conduct throughout the Middle East in places like

Syria, Lebanon, Yemen, has demonstrated that they are very much a malevolent force.

And I think I join both my colleagues in supporting the need for us to move very swiftly on tough sanctions, both again Iran's ballistic missile program and against the Revolutionary Guard Corps.

And I yield back the balance of my time.

Ms. ROS-LEHTINEN. Thank you very much, Mr. DeSantis.

Mr. Boyle of Pennsylvania.

Mr. BOYLE. Thank you, and I will be brief. Some of this will be a little bit repetitive from what Mr. Deutch was saying.

Essentially the intelligence community has assessed that Iran has the largest inventory of ballistic missiles in the Middle East. U.N. Security Council Resolution 2231 calls upon Iran—and let me quote it specifically, because I think this is sometimes confused by some, "not to undertake any activity related to ballistic missiles designed to be capable of delivering nuclear weapons, including launches using ballistic missiles technology."

Despite that, we know now there have been some 15 illegal tests since 2231 came into force. So I look forward to this hearing and specifically discussing ways we can move forward on this matter that do not in any way conflict with the JCPOA, but live up to the letter of the law of 2231.

Thank you. I yield back.

Ms. ROS-LEHTINEN. Thank you Mr. Boyle.

Mr. Mast of Florida.

Mr. MAST. Thank you, Chairman.

You know, as we speak about this issue, I just ask that we always keep into perspective what we have allowed to become very cliche, in that we constantly point to Iran using the phrase "the largest state sponsor of terror," and ask ourselves, what does that really mean?

For those of us that have spent time on our Nation's battlefields in modern history, we know exactly that that looks like. It was Iranian hands that produced improvised explosive devices that literally killed thousands of our servicemembers in Iraq. It was Iranian hands that packed improvised explosive devises with nuts and screws and bolts and other pieces of shrapnel so that they would put so many holes in our servicemembers that we couldn't plug each and every one of them before they would hemorrhage out. That's the enemy that we are dealing with. As my colleague, Mr. Deutch, put it, the group that is sowing instability. That is how they sow that instability. And I ask that we keep that in perspective as we move forward in this dialogue.

Thank you.

Ms. ROS-LEHTINEN. Thank you, sir, for your service.

Mr. Schneider of Illinois.

Mr. SCHNEIDER. Thank you, Madam Chairman. I want to thank you and the ranking member for calling this very important hearing. I thank the witnesses for sharing their perspectives and insights.

Iran obviously remains a significant threat in the region, around the world, to our allies and to our interests. And while a nuclear Iran is without question one of the greatest threats we could face, Iran continues to, through its ballistic missile development, through its shipment of conventional arms, through its nefarious activities in the region, in the world, and as well as its violations of human rights, to remain a very bad actor.

As the ranking member said, the JCPOA does not preclude us from taking actions to thwart Iran's ballistic missile program or to address their other nefarious actions around the world and in the region. I would take it a step further in fact: I believe we have a moral obligation to do just that. And I look forward to have this hearing to talk about how we can push back on Iran's behavior.

Thank you, and I yield back.

Ms. ROS-LEHTINEN. Thank you, sir.

Mr. Fitzpatrick of Pennsylvania.

Mr. FITZPATRICK. Thank you, Madam Chairman.

As a former FBI agent dealing with counterterrorism matters, it was often our job to find the nexus between terrorists and their state sponsors. And since the 1980s, the largest and most adept state sponsor of terrorism has been the Islamic Republic of Iran. Americans first became aware of this somber fact back in 1983 when an Iranian-sponsored terrorist group, Hezbollah, bombed the Marine barracks in Beirut, Lebanon.

Since then, Iran has continued to support groups that target Americans abroad. From 1982 to 1992, Iranian-backed Hezbollah kidnapped and held captive some 104 hostages in Lebanon, including the CIA's Beirut station chief, William Buckley. After the invasions of Afghanistan and Iraq, Iranian intelligence and Revolutionary Guard Corps operatives provided training, arms, IED materials to insurgents.

In recent years, the Iranian Revolutionary Guard Corps, specifically the shadowy Quds Force group, has attempted to sow continued instability throughout the Middle East. In Syria, the IRGC advisers have fought and died alongside of the forces of Bashar al-Assad.

In Iraq, the commander of the Quds Force has been seen advising and assisting local Iraqi Shiite militias. Some of these militias, such as the Badr organization, have been accused of heinous human rights abuses. These militias have worsened the already heightened sectarianism between the Sunnis and Shiites in Iraq.

Unfortunately, Iran's treachery has not been met with any increased sanctions or diplomatic pressure. Rather in recent years they have been awarded over $1 billion in frozen assets to Iran as part of the Joint Comprehensive Plan of Action, otherwise known as the JCPOA.

The JCPOA has not only upset America's Sunni Arab allies, it has also emboldened Iran. Iran still continues to test ballistic missiles and continues to sow discord and sectarianism throughout the region. While it is important to continue the fight against ISIS in Iraq and Syria, we must remain vigilant and prevent Iran from establishing a crescent of influence throughout the region.

I yield back, Madam Chairman.

Ms. ROS-LEHTINEN. Thank you, sir.

Mr. Cicilline.

Mr. CICILLINE. Thank you, Chairman Ros-Lehtinen and Ranking Member Deutch, for holding this important hearing on Iran's ballistic missile program.

Without question, Iran's continued efforts to develop short-range and medium-range ballistic missiles and its ambition to develop intercontinental ballistic missiles pose a significant challenge to the United States and our allies. Development of these capabilities pose significant risks to U.S. forces and interests in the region, and it is also places Israel and our allies in the Persian Gulf in danger. Iran cannot be allowed to define international agreements and create increased uncertainty and disorder in the Middle East. At the same time, I believe it is essential that our response to Iran's defiance of international agreements not undermine the progress made under the Joint Comprehensive Plan of Action to curb Iran's nuclear program.

It is my hope that the Trump administration will continue to work closely with our partners and allies to address the mutual challenges posed by Iran. I look forward to hearing from today's witnesses and hearing their insights on how to best respond to Iran's continued development of its ballistic missile program while ensuring that we do not move backwards in the international effort to prevent Iran from obtaining nuclear weapons.

And with that, I thank the gentlelady and yield back.

Ms. ROS-LEHTINEN. Thank Mr. Cicilline.

And now we turn to Mrs. Wagner of Missouri.

Mrs. WAGNER. Thank you, Madam Chairman.

Last month a senior member of the Iranian Parliament's National Security and Foreign Policy Commission warned us that had the U.S. Army's Fifth Fleet in Bahrain will be, and I quote, "razed to the ground if the enemy," the United States, "makes a mistake." These comments are particularly threatening in light of Iranian's denial of confrontations between its fast attack boats and U.S. ships in the Gulf last week.

It is clear that Iran interprets reality, their own reality, however, as it chooses, and future incidents could easily end in shots fired. Iran is one of the United States' most severe security threats and the JCPOA—or, as we would call it, the Iran deal—has done little to mitigate dangerous conflict.

I look forward to discussing this afternoon how we can best reduce tensions in the region and hold Iran accountable for its actions.

And I thank you, Madam Chairman.

Ms. ROS-LEHTINEN. Thank you for an excellent statement.

And now I am pleased to introduce our witnesses this afternoon. First, we are delighted to welcome back Dr. Kenneth Katzman, who serves as the senior Middle East analyst for the Congressional Research Service. He is a specialist on Iran, on the Persian Gulf states, and Afghanistan. Dr. Katzman is also an expert on Iran's Islamic Revolutionary Guard Corps, the IRGC, and he has written one of the preeminent books on the subject and is an expert on Iranian-backed groups operating in the Middle East. Prior to this, he was an analyst at the CIA. He is a foremost expert on Iran's Revolutionary Guard.

We look forward once again to your testimony, Dr. Katzman. Welcome back.

Next, we want to also welcome back Mr. Michael Eisenstadt. He is the director of the Military and Securities Study Program at the

Washington Institute for Near East Policy. Prior to joining the institute, he served for 26 years as an officer in the U.S. Army Reserve.

Thank you for your service, sir, and we look forward to your testimony, Mr. Eisenstadt.

Finally, we would like to welcome Elizabeth Rosenberg, director of the Energy, Economics and Security Program at the Center for a New American Security. She served as a senior adviser to the U.S. Department of the Treasury, to the assistant secretary for terrorist financing and financial crimes, and then to the under secretary for terrorism financial intelligence. In these roles she has worked on tightening global sanctions on Iran.

Welcome to our subcommittee, Ms. Rosenberg.

And as I stated in my opening statement, your full statements will be made a part of the record. Please feel free to synthesize. Thank you.

Dr. Katzman, we will begin with you while I clean up here.

STATEMENT OF KENNETH KATZMAN, PH.D., SPECIALIST IN MIDDLE EASTERN AFFAIRS, CONGRESSIONAL RESEARCH SERVICE

Mr. KATZMAN. Thank you, Madam Chairwoman. And thank you, Mr. Deutch, for inviting CRS to testify today. I will summarize my statement. I ask that my full statement, which was cleared by the CRS review process, be included in the record.

First, I will talk a little about what are Iran's objectives in its ballistic missile program. We think it is multifaceted: Iran's long-standing national identity, Iran's ideology, a response to perceived threats, and domestic political dynamics in Iran.

In terms of national prestige and pride, developing a large sophisticated missile arsenal enhances Iran's prestige and international reputation.

Ideologically, the transfer by the Quds Force, as was mentioned, the IRGC Quds Force, of shorter-range missiles and rockets to forces in the region, such as Hezbollah, Hamas, the Houthis in Yemen, appears to be aimed at boosting movements that share Iran's ideology, which is ultimately to overturn a power structure in the region that Iran's leaders feel was established by and serves the United States, Israel, and Saudi Arabia.

Strategically, Iran's missile program can be interpreted as an equalizer to address Iran's conventional military weaknesses relative to the United States or any other regional power. Iran's supply of short-range missiles to Hezbollah, for example, gives Iran and Hezbollah the option to attack Israel. Iran's shipments to the Houthis in Yemen, which they have used on several occasions, position Iran to project power not only in the Gulf, where it traditionally projects power, but also now on the southern coast of the Arabian Peninsula.

In terms of Iranian politics, Iran's President Hassan Rouhani might perceive that because he was the architect on the Iranian side of the JCPOA, he might be vulnerable to hardline elements who might ask him, "Well, you have given up Iran's nuclear deterrent potential, how do you plan to defend the country?" And missiles could be seen as his answer to that challenge.

On the IRGC, the ballistic missile program, as was noted, is run by the IRGC Air Force. The IRGC Air Force originally was designed to become an air force, but Iran quickly learned that it was too expensive and too time consuming to develop another air force alongside the regular air force, so they assigned the IRGC Air Force to handle Iran's ballistic missile program.

The Quds Force, as was noted, is a key instrument in Iran's attempts to reshape regional politics to its advantage through these weapons transfers of cruise short-range missiles.

The IRGC also, because its charter is to defend the revolution, it interprets its mission as justifying its involvement in Iranian politics, which is really unique to militaries around the world. It is one of the only—I haven't studied all of the militaries in the world—but it is one of the only militaries that says its mission is to involve itself in politics.

The IRGC Navy is amply supplied with cruise and coastal defense missiles, mostly purchased from outside suppliers. The IRGC Navy and the regular navy, again two navies, IRGC Navy and a regular navy, use these missiles to try to control Iran's territorial waters.

Sanctions and others options. The JCPOA imposes no restrictions on Iran's missile program. U.N. Security Council Resolution 2231 calls upon Iran to refrain for a maximum of 8 years from developing ballistic missiles designed to be capable of delivering nuclear weapons. And that is 8 years from October 2015, so we are now really 6½ years until that restriction expires.

There are a number of options available to the Trump administration to counter Iran's ballistic missile program. One option is additional sanctions. At their height in 2012-2013, sanctions had significant effect on Iran's economy and clearly contributed to its acceptance of the JCPOA. Yet, Iran continued to expand its nuclear and missile programs.

One problem is the JCPOA essentially walls off Iran's main economic sectors from new sanctions, because there is language that Iran would consider it a breach if sanctions are reimposed, the ones that were lifted are reimposed, which makes it difficult, we think, to impose new proliferation-related sanctions, which would not touch the main economic sectors. If you don't touch Iran's main economic sectors, it might be hard to be effective in changing Iran's calculations.

Another option would be to designate the IRGC as a foreign terrorist organization. It is difficult, however, to see how much additional actual pressure this would add on the IRGC that is not already imposed under existing sanctions, which are extensive on the IRGC.

Other options could be enhancing U.S. and regional missile defense. And as far as military options, President Trump has said that all options are on the table, but he has not specified criteria or circumstances that could trigger potential U.S. military action on Iran.

I look forward to your questions. Thank you.

[The prepared statement of Mr. Katzman follows:]

Congressional Research Service
Informing the legislative debate since 1914

TESTIMONY

Statement of

Kenneth Katzman
Specialist in Middle Eastern Affairs

Before

Committee on Foreign Affairs
Subcommittee on Middle East and North Africa

Hearing on

"Testing the Limits: Iran's Ballistic Missile Program, Sanctions, and the Islamic Revolutionary Guard Corps"

March 29, 2017

Congressional Research Service
7-5700
www.crs.gov
<Product Code>

Search Terms

IRGC, Iran, missile, sanctions, Revolutionary Guard, INKSNA, Rouhani, Khamene'i, IRGC-Qods Force, Hezbollah, Hamas, Israel, Persian Gulf, GCC.

I thank the chairpersons and ranking Members of the subcommittee for inviting CRS to provide testimony for today's hearing. I will summarize my statement and ask that my full statement be included in the record.

I have been asked to testify today on the objectives of Iran's missile programs and systems, and related Revolutionary Guard and sanctions issues. I will confine my testimony to those issues, and not address the highly technical issues of Iran's missile systems and related U.S. and other countermeasures that might determine whether Iran's missile programs are capable of achieving Iran's objectives.

U.S. Policy Context for Considering Iran's Missile Program

The first few months of the Trump Administration provide a lens through which to assess the objectives of Iran's missile program. The new Administration has reverted to the U.S. characterization of Iran that has prevailed for most of the time since the 1979 revolution – Iran as an adversary that is incligible to become a partner in resolving regional conflicts. Trump Administration officials do not articulate a future relationship with Iran in which U.S.-Iran animosity and hostility is put aside in favor of a constructive relationship. On February 1, the Trump Administration announced that it was "officially putting Iran on notice" for recent actions that "threaten U.S. friends and allies in the region," including the January 29 test of a ballistic missile and "weapons transfers [to groups such as the Houthi rebels in Yemen], support for terrorism, and other violations of international norms."[1]

Another significant consideration for evaluating Iran's missile program is the July 2015 multilateral nuclear agreement with Iran, the Joint Comprehensive Plan of Action (JCPOA), does not restrict Iran's ballistic missile programs. U.N. Security Council Resolution 2231,[2] which endorses the JCPOA and supersedes all previous Iran resolutions, prohibits Iran from exporting weaponry and "call[s] upon" - but does not require - Iran "not to undertake any activity related to ballistic missiles designed to be capable of delivering nuclear weapons, including launches...." Yet, Iran has conducted several ballistic missile tests since JCPOA "Implementation Day" on January 16, 2016—the day Resolution 2231 formally took effect.

Objectives of Iran's Missile Programs

U.S. officials assert that Iran has a growing and increasingly sophisticated arsenal of missiles of varied ranges and types. These missiles appear to pose a potential threat to U.S. allies in the region, including Israel, as well as to U.S. ships, armed forces, and allies in the Persian Gulf. To varying degrees, Iran is at odds with the six Gulf states that are run by Sunni Arab-led monarchies who are allied in the Gulf Cooperation Council (GCC)[3]

Iran's decision to develop missiles of ever larger number and sophistication is the product of many, and sometimes competing, factors: Iran's long-standing Iranian national interests; the ideology of Iran's Islamic revolution; as a response to Iranian leaders' perceived threats to the regime and to the country; and interaction among the Iranian regime's domestic political dynamics.

---

[1] The text of then-National Security Adviser Michael Flynn's statement on Iran can be found at:
https://www.whitehouse.gov/the-press-office/2017/02/01/statement-national-security-advisor

[2] The text of the resolution can be found at: http://www.un.org/en/ga/search/view_doc.asp?symbol=S/RES/2231%282015%29

[3] The GCC consist of: Saudi Arabia, Kuwait, United Arab Emirates, Qatar, Bahrain, and Oman.

Long-standing National Identity

Iranian leaders assert that Iran's long Persian Gulf coastline entitles the country to a major say in Gulf security arrangements. Iran's leaders argue that Iran has an ancient, historical civilization, often contrasting its past with that of the smaller Gulf states, most of which regained independence only in the 1960s or 1970s. Iran's assertions of a right to a significant "seat at the table" in the Gulf are similar, in many respects, to those made by the Shah of Iran, who was toppled by the 1979 revolution. The Shah was a close U.S. ally and his attempts to dominate the Persian Gulf region were largely supported by, or at the very least not vigorously opposed by, the United States. In large part because of the nearly 40 years of U.S.-Iran animosity, even policies of the current regime that are similar to those of the Shah are key factors in U.S. criticism of Iranian policy.

Iran's development of an advanced missile arsenal grew out of a plan to respond to Iraqi missile attacks on Iranian cities during the 1980-88 Iran-Iraq War, and now supports Iran's assertions of geographic and historical primacy in the region. Developing a sophisticated missile arsenal might enhance Iran's international prestige and contributes to the regime's efforts to restore a sense of "greatness" reminiscent of past Persian empires or ruling dynasties. Iran might also see its missile program as enhancing its reputation as a growing advanced industrial power. In particular, Iran's space launch and satellite programs might be intended to serve the above objectives.

Ideology

Iranian leaders routinely assert that the existing power structure in the Middle East has been established by - and favors - the United States, Israel, and Saudi Arabia. Iranian leaders assert that these powers and their allies, in an effort to remain dominant in the region, marginalize Shiite Muslims and Islamist movements that might seek to challenge incumbent regimes or U.S. influence in the region. Furthermore, Saudi Arabia, in particular, through such actions as intervening militarily in Yemen against the Houthis and supporting Sunni rebels in Yemen, is instigating sectarian tensions and trying to significantly curtail Iran's regional influence.

The reported transfer by Iran of shorter-range missiles and rockets to forces in the region such as Hezbollah, Hamas, and the Houthis in Yemen appears to be aimed at enhancing Iran's ability to protect allies that share and can help Iran implement its regional policies. In virtually all cases, factions to which Iran provides rockets and short-range missiles oppose Israel, Saudi Arabia and the other Gulf states, and the United States.

Iranian leaders also assert a sense of "victimhood," which serves as a further possible explanation for Iran's extensive missile development efforts. Some analysts consider Iran's missile program as "Iran's answer to the legacy of Saddam Hussein's missiles raining down on Iranian cities during a brutal eight year war with Iraq (Iran – Iraq War)."[4] Iranian leaders also repeatedly cite that their country was a victim of the use of chemical weapons use by Iraq during that war.

Response to Perceived Threats

Iran's ballistic missile programs can be interpreted primarily as a strategic deterrent—an attempt to wield countervailing power should the United States or any other country invade Iran or try to intimidate it or to change its regime. Iranian missile attacks against U.S. bases, while not likely to be militarily decisive, could disrupt or complicate (but not halt) base operations. Iran's Supreme Leader, Grand Ayatollah Ali Khamene'i, expressed Iran's motivation for developing ballistic missiles as follows:

[4] Bharath Gopalaswamy and Amir Handjani. "Get Real on Iran's Missile Program." War on the Rocks, March 15, 2017.

If the Islamic establishment seeks technology and negotiations but does not have defensive power, it will have to back down in the face of any petty country that appears as a threat.[5]

Further, following a ballistic missile test in 2016, the head of Iran's missile programs stated that the test was intended "to show Iran's deterrent power and also the Islamic Republic's ability to confront any threat against the [Islamic] Revolution, the state and the sovereignty of the country."[6]

Iranian leaders appear to see ballistic missiles as an "equalizer"—a means of addressing Iran's conventional military weaknesses against the United States. And because U.N. Security Council Resolution 2231 – which I will discuss further below - continued a virtual ban, for up to five years, on importation by Iran of conventional arms, Iran has few means to maintain its military capability against neighbors that spend far more on defense than does Iran and which are supplied with modern, advanced weapons systems by the United States and other major weapons suppliers.[7]

Iran's short-range missile systems and acquisitions also appear intended, at least in part, for battlefield and tactical military purposes, including supporting Iran's efforts to control—or deny adversaries access to—the waterways around Iran. Successive National Defense Authorization Acts (NDAAs) have required an annual report on Iran's military power. The unclassified summary of the latest available report, dated January 2016, states that "Iran continues to develop capabilities to defend its homeland and to control avenues of approach, to include the Strait of Hormuz, in the event of a military conflict."[8]

Iran also equips Hezbollah with short-range missiles to provide additional options to respond to any attack on Iran's nuclear facilities or other assets. As part of any Iranian response, Hezbollah, either directed by Tehran or independently, could inflict significant casualties on Israel. Iran's missile-wielding regional partners are also positioned to help Tehran internationalize any U.S. – Iran, Saudi – Iran, or other bilateral conflict with Iran.

Iran's apparent transfers of anti-ship missiles to the Houthis in Yemen - which the Houthis have used on several occasions against U.S. and Gulf state ships – could position Iran to try to project power into the key maritime chokepoint on the southern coast of the Arabian Peninsula. U.S. officials have stated that Iran supplies arms to the Houthis but there is debate about the degree of influence Tehran has on Houthi operations.[9] The Houthi missile deployments in Yemen cannot, therefore, necessarily be interpreted as power projected by Tehran.

Domestic Political Dynamics

Iran's domestic politics might also be a factor in Iran's decisions about its missile program. Iran's President Hassan Rouhani, who faces a re-election vote in May, is extensively identified with the JCPOA, in which Iran pledged to never seek to develop a nuclear weapon in exchange for sanctions relief. Rouhani might perceive that he could be politically vulnerable to hardline elements who charge that after foregoing Iran's potential to develop a nuclear deterrent, the country should at least have an alternative deterrent strategy. The hardline camp includes not only the Supreme Leader but also the Islamic Revolutionary Guard Corps (IRGC, discussed further below). Rouhani might see the development of a sophisticated and large missile arsenal as satisfying that political requirement. Supporting continued

---

[5] "Supreme Leader: Iran Should Strengthen Capabilities for Defense." Fars News Agency, March 30, 3016.

[6] Reuters, March 9, 2016. http://www.reuters.com/article/us-iran-missiles-idUSKCN0WA0UY

[7] "Get Real on Iran's Missile Program." op.cit.

[8] Department of Defense. Unclassified Executive Summary. "Annual Report on Military Power of Iran." January 2016. The FY2016 NDAA (P.L. 114-92) extended the annual DOD reporting requirement until the end of 2025.

[9] Marieke Transfeld. "Iran's Small Hand in Yemen." Carnegie Endowment, February 14, 2017. http://carnegieendowment.org/sada/67988

missile development might also help Rouhani parry recent criticism from hardliners that the JCPOA has produced economic benefits that are far more modest than what was anticipated.

The Revolutionary Guard and Iran's Missile Programs

An assessment of Iran's objectives in developing ballistic missile technology is linked to how the ballistic missile program is run and how that program relates to Iran's political hierarchy. Iran's ballistic missile program is run by a sub- unit of the politically powerful IRGC.[10][11] The IRGC is the force that was formed from armed elements that overthrew the Shah's government in 1979. It plays a key role in virtually all of the regime's foreign policy and in maintaining internal security. The IRGC's role, direct and indirect, in Iran's economy has grown significantly over the past twenty years as former IRGC officers have used their connections to regime leaders to win contracts and expand corporate entities in many different industries. The IRGC not only runs Iran's missile development program, but also transfers short-range ballistic missiles to Iran's regional allies and proxies.

Organizationally, the IRGC is part of a broader Iranian armed forces structure that assigns functions to different forces as appropriate to their roles. The IRGC's formal mission, assigned to the force when it was established in 1979, is to defend the revolution—a role its commanders interpret as defending the regime from any threat, external or internal. As part of that overall charter, the IRGC also has a national defense role alongside the regular military (*Artesh*), the national army that existed under the former Shah. Both the IRGC and the regular military report to a joint headquarters headed since June 2016 by IRGC Major General Mohammad Hossein Bagheri. The fact that the joint headquarters is headed by an IRGC senior officer demonstrates the paramount role the regime assigns to the IRGC in comparison to the regular military. Since its establishment, the IRGC has established subunits, including ground forces, a navy, and an air force, that generally parallel similar services of the regular military. Public sources indicate that the IRGC has approximately 125,000 personnel, but that figure does not include the Basij militia that it controls.

IRGC Internal Security and Political Role

The IRGC has broader functions than national defense. The IRGC controls the *Basij* (Mobilization of the Oppressed and Disabled) volunteer militia that has been the main instrument for repressing domestic dissent. When fully mobilized—and it tends to fully mobilize on an as-needed basis—the Basij might field several hundred thousand personnel. The regular military, deployed mainly at bases outside major cities, does not have a mandate to undertake political action such as suppressing unrest and public demonstrations, and its leadership has repeatedly stated that it would not engage in internal security activities even if directed to do so by the regime.

IRGC senior leaders assert that the IRGC's mission of defending the revolution justifies expressing its views on national decisions and national politics. The IRGC, largely through the Basij militia, was widely reported to have orchestrated support for former President Mahmoud Ahmadinejad in the 2005 and 2009 elections, the latter of which sparked more than a year of major protests against regime fraud in that election. The IRGC, acting through its command of the Basij, played the leading role in suppressing the demonstrations and containing and ultimately crushing the uprising. Apparently concerned that the IRGC

---

[10] For an extensive discussion of the IRGC and its missions, see Katzman, Kenneth, "The Warriors of Islam: Iran's Revolutionary Guard," *Westview Press*, 1993.

[11] The IRGC is known in Persian language as the *Sepah-e-Pasdaran Enghelab Islami*).

and Basij might again interfere on behalf of hardline opponents in the May 19, 2017 presidential election, President Rouhani stated:[12]

> We all have to be careful that government resources are not used in favor of one individual or party. This is a sin. By government, I mean the executive, the judiciary, the armed forces. I mean all the organizations that use public funds. No one has a right to use a public platform, public media, newspaper or website that uses public funds in the election.

In mid-March 2017, the Commander-in Chief of the IRGC, IRGC Major General Mohammad Ali Jafari, appeared to join other hardline criticism of President Rouhani, saying that "many officials... governing the country now... have a Western, liberal, and un-revolutionary viewpoint.[13] This statement raises concerns that the IRGC might, as it did in the 2005 and 2009 elections, intervene on behalf of hardline challengers in the upcoming election, despite Rouhani's warning.

The IRGC Foreign Policy Role: the Qods Force

The IRGC also has a foreign policy role that the regular military does not. The IRGC has a unit, the IRGC–Qods Force (IRGC-QF, *Qods* means Jerusalem), whose task is to provide material support to pro-Iranian movements and governments in the region. In performing that mission, the IRGC-QF is a key Iranian government instrument in its attempts to reshape regional politics to Iran's advantage. The IRGC-QF, which has an estimated 20,000 personnel serving in various locations in the region as well as further afield, is headed by IRGC Major General Qasem Soleimani, who reports directly to Khamene'i.[14] IRGC leaders have on numerous occasions publicly acknowledged these activities; on August 20, 2016, an IRGC-QF commander in Syria told an Iranian newspaper that Iran had formed a "Liberation Army" consisting of local, mostly Shiite, fighters that support Iran's interests in various Arab countries.[15] Much of the weaponry Iran supplies to its allies include specialized anti-tank systems, artillery rockets, mortars, and short-range missiles.[16] Close ties between the IRGC-QF and some Shiite militia forces in Iraq complicates U.S. policy decisions in that country.

Until recently, we had not seen reports of the regular military operating outside Iran's borders. However, apparently as part of Iran's push to help Syrian President Bashar Al Asad recapture rebel-held parts of Aleppo, some regular ground forces (Islamic Republic of Iran Ground Forces, IRIGF) were deployed to Syria. The IRGC-QF most likely assessed that the IRIGF expertise in conventional warfare would be useful in helping Syrian army forces.

The IRGC Air Force's Role in Iran's Missile Program

As part of its efforts to develop services at least equal in capability to those of the regular military, the IRGC established its Air Force in the late 1980s. However, establishing a new air force is capital intensive, including acquisition of aircraft, training of pilots, and development of maintenance facilities. Several years after establishing the IRGC Air Force, the IRGC and Iran's civilian leadership largely

---

[12] "Iran's Rouhani Warns Military Not to Intervene in Elections." Al Monitor. February 27, 2017. http://www.al-monitor.com/pulse/originals/2017/02/iran-rouhani-criticism-electoral-interference-conservatives.html

[13] Comments by Jafari in Fars News, translated by American Enterprise Institute "Critical Threats Project" Published by AEI on March 17, 2017. http://www.farsnews.com/13951225000340

[14] Dexter Filkins. "The Shadow Commander," *The New Yorker*, September 30, 2013. http://www.newyorker.com/reporting/2013/09/30/130930fa_fact_filkins?printable=true&currentPage=all

[15] Al Jazeera. August 20, 2016.

[16] Farzin Nadimi. "How Iran's Revived Weapons Exports Could Boost its Proxies." Washington Institute for Near East Policy, August 17, 2015.

discontinued the IRGC Air Force's efforts to build out a separate conventional air capability, and instead assigned the force to run Iran's missile programs.

The commander of the IRGC Air Force, an officer who often comments on Iran's missile tests and development programs, is IRGC Brigadier General Amir Ali Hajizadeh. He is widely considered a hardliner who opposes negotiations with the United States on regional issues and who argues against limiting Iran's missile development in response to U.S. threats or sanctions.[17] According to the Department of the Treasury, the IRGC Air Force entity that has operational control over Iran's missile program is the Al Ghadir Missile Command.[18] The missile command was first designated, and subjected to sanctions, as a "proliferation supporting entity" by the Treasury Department in 2010, under Executive Order 13382. (The IRGC itself was designated under that Order in 2007.) Also identified under that Order, is the Shahid Hemmat Industrial Group (SHIG), a key contractor to Iran's missile program. Numerous entities affiliated with or performing work for SHIG have been designated under the Order.

On November 12, 2011, the senior IRGC Air Force commander of a ballistic missile base outside Tehran was killed by a large explosion that destroyed the entire base. Iranian leaders blamed mishandling of missile fuel for the explosion, denying reports of internal subterfuge. The explosion temporarily set back Iran's missile development program.

The IRGC Navy's Role in the Missile Program

The IRGC Navy, headed since 2010 by IRGC Rear Admiral Ali Fadavi, has emerged as one of the IRGC's most potent units. It has been amply supplied with cruise and coastal defense missiles, some developed by Iran but most purchased from outside suppliers. According to the U.S. Office of Naval Intelligence, both the IRGC Navy and the Islamic Republic of Iran Navy (IRIN, regular navy) are fielding a growing arsenal of cruise and short range ballistic missiles in order to "control Iran's maritime environment."[19]

One missile in the arsenal is the China-supplied C-802 sea-skimming cruise missile, which has also reportedly been transferred to Iran's regional allies. Iran bought large numbers of these missiles in the early 1990s to outfit patrol boats it bought from China as well as other small boats operated by the IRGC Navy. The IRGC-QF reportedly re-transferred some of these missiles to Hezbollah, which used the weapon against an Israeli ship in the 2006 Israel-Hezbollah war, causing severe damage to the vessel.[20] The Houthi rebels in Yemen might also be a recipient of C-802 re-transfers; the Houthis reportedly used the weapon in attacks on a UAE and a U.S. ship in the Red Sea in late 2016. The attacks damaged the UAE ship but, apparently because of U.S. countermeasures, did not damage the U.S. ship.[21]

The IRGC Navy appears to be a pivotal component of Tehran's strategy to assert its power in the Persian Gulf and fully intends to defend what it considers its territorial waters. Over the past few years, and as recently as early March 2017, the IRGC Navy has conducted so-called "high speed intercepts" of U.S. naval vessels in the Gulf. In some cases, the United States has responded by firing "warning shots" that caused the Iranian vessels to break off the encounter. No actual hostilities have resulted from these

---

[17] Translations of Hajizadeh comments quoted in American Enterprise Institute "Iran Tracker." March 10, 2017.

[18] https://www.treasury.gov/press-center/press-releases/Pages/jl0395.aspx

[19] Office of Naval Intelligence. "Iranian Naval Forces: A Tale of Two Navies." Released March 1, 2017.
http://www.oni.navy.mil/Portals/12/Intel%20agencies/iran/Iran%200222217S.pdf?ver=2017-02-28-082613-220

[20] "Arming of Hezbollah Reveals U.S. and Israeli Blind Spots." New York Times, July 19, 2006.
http://www.nytimes.com/2006/07/19/world/middleeast/19missile.html

[21] Sam Legrone. "U.S.S. Mason Fired 3 Missiles to Defend From Yemen Cruise Missile Attack. USNI (U.S. Naval Institute) News, October 11, 2016. https://news.usni.org/2016/10/11/uss-mason-fired-3-missiles-to-defend-from-yemen-cruise-missiles-attack

18

incidents, although in January 2016, the IRGC Navy took into custody and held for one day ten U.S. Navy personnel that strayed off course into what Iran called its territorial waters. U.S. officials have called the high speed intercepts "unprofessional" and "unsafe."[22] U.S. officials have also said that Iran claims as its territorial waters areas that the United States regards as international waters under international maritime law.

U.S. Responses, Options, and Sanctions Issues

The options available to the Administration to counter Iran's missile program and the regional activities carried out by the IRGC-QF are, to some extent, constrained by the JCPOA and the relaxation of U.N. restrictions on Iran's missile program that accompanied the JCPOA. The JCPOA itself contains no specific requirements or restrictions on Iran with respect to ballistic or any other missile programs. U.N. Security Council Resolution 2231, which took effect on Implementation Day and supersedes all previous Iran-related resolutions, "calls upon" (but does not require) Iran to refrain from developing or testing ballistic missiles "designed to be capable of delivering nuclear weapons" until the earlier of: October 2023, or when the International Atomic Energy Agency (IAEA) reaches a "Broader Conclusion" that Iran's nuclear activities can only be used for purely peaceful purposes.

The essentially voluntary nature of Resolution 2231 contrasts with language in Resolution 1929 of June 2010, which Resolution 2231 superseded. Resolution 1929 provided for a mandatory ban on Iran's development of ballistic missiles, stating that the U.N. Security Council:

> *Decides* that Iran *shall not* undertake any activity related to ballistic missiles *capable of* delivering nuclear weapons, including launches using ballistic missile technology (emphasis added)...

Neither Resolution 2231 nor the JCPOA contains any specific limitations or commitments with respect to the IRGC's regional actions and operations; however, Resolution 2231 continued provisions, placed on Iran in previous Resolutions (1737 and 1747), barring Iran from exporting arms or importing conventional weapons systems.

Resolution 2231 requires that, for five years from Adoption Day (until October 2020), or until a Broader Conclusion is reached, any Iranian importation or exportation of arms requires Security Council approval. Nevertheless, because the United States has a veto on the U.N. Security Council, such arms transactions by Iran are essentially prohibited, because U.S. officials have stated consistent opposition to new purchases of arms by Iran. And yet, the expiration of the restriction means that, three and half years from now, Iran will be able to import or export arms without violating any Iran-related U.N. requirement.

Iran Placed "On Notice"

On February 1, 2017, subsequent to Iran's January 29, 2017 test of a ballistic missile—the first ballistic missile test Iran conducted since the new Administration took office—the Trump Administration announced that it was "officially putting Iran on notice" for recent actions that "threaten U.S. friends and allies in the region," including the missile test and "weapons transfers [to groups such as Houthi rebels in Yemen], support for terrorism, and other violations of international norms."[23] Administration officials said the Administration was undertaking a "deliberative process" to formulate responses to such Iranian actions.[24] Trump Administration officials stated that the U.S. response to Iran's missile test and its

---

[22] ABC News, September 6, 2016. http://abcnews.go.com/International/iranian-boats-harass-navy-ship-gulf/story?id=41896528
[23] The text of then-National Security Adviser Michael Flynn's statement on Iran can be found at: https://www.whitehouse.gov/the-press-office/2017/02/01/statement-national-security-advisor
[24] "White House in 'Deliberative Process' to Form Response to Iran Missile Test." Washington Examiner, February 1, 2017. http://www.washingtonexaminer.com/white-house-in-deliberative-process-to-form-response-to-iran-missile-test/article/2613654

regional "malign activities" would be separate from and not in conflict with U.S. commitments in the JCPOA.

The Administration characterized the Iranian missile test in terms similar to those used by the Obama Administration in 2016 (after Resolution 2231 took effect) as being "in defiance of" Resolution 2231 and as "destabilizing and provocative," but not a "violation" of Resolution 2231. The post-Implementation Day tests might not be considered a violation because of Resolution 2231's characterization of the restriction on Iranian missile development as voluntary. For their part, Iranian leaders have argued that their recent missile tests are consistent with Resolution 2231 because Iran, in the JCPOA, commits to not developing a nuclear weapon. Therefore, according to the Iranian argument, Iran would not have intent to design a missile to carry a nuclear payload.[25]

In terms of an international response, the Trump Administration followed a process at the United Nations similar to that used by the Obama Administration following Iran's March 2016 missile tests. The Trump Administration called for a U.N. Security Council meeting to determine whether the tests violated Resolution 2231 and the Council, as it did in 2016, referred the issue to its sanctions committee.

Sanctions Implementation and Options

U.N. resolutions and U.S. and international sanctions have had little observable effect on Iran's missile program or its regional interventions. U.S. secondary sanctions and multilateral sanctions imposed on Iran during 2010-2013 had a significant effect on Iran's economy and, by most accounts, contributed significantly to Iran's decision to negotiate the JCPOA. However, even during this period, Iran significantly expanded and enhanced its nuclear program's capabilities. Similarly, Iran was able to develop its ballistic missile programs, although the sanctions—coupled with multilateral calculations about the risks of helping Iran's strategic programs—may have caused some countries to refrain from selling Iran missile systems and conventional weapons. Iranian leaders assert that Iran's missile and space launches will continue no matter how the United States, United Nations, or any other nations respond.

The JCPOA did not commit the United States to lift or suspend sanctions against Iranian proliferation activities, and several U.S. laws and Executive Orders authorize U.S. sanctions against foreign entities that support Iran's missile program, and other strategic weapons programs. However, the JCPOA states:

> Iran has stated that it will treat such a re-introduction or re-imposition of the sanctions specified in Annex II (those sanctions the U.S. has lifted or waived), or such an imposition of new nuclear-related sanctions, as grounds to cease performing its commitments under this JCPOA in whole or in part.

The interpretation of the JCPOA statement among experts and U.S. and other officials is that Iran's core economic sectors—including energy, banking, shipping, shipping insurance, manufacturing, auto production, and others—are essentially "walled off" from new or re-imposed U.S. secondary sanctions. It can be argued that this restriction limits the U.S. ability to impose any new sanctions on Iran that would have significant effect in compelling Iran to agree to limits to its missile program, regional activities, or other behaviors. Sanctions that have been effective on Iran, to date, have generally targeted those key sectors by forcing third country firms to choose between doing business in Iran and doing business in the U.S. market.

---

[25]Al Jazeera News Network. January 31, 2017. http://www.aljazeera.com/news/2017/01/iran-missile-tests-violation-nuclear-deal-170131103418904.html

Executive Orders 13382 and 13224

One tool that recent Administrations, including the Trump Administration, have utilized to counter Iran's missile program has been to impose sanctions in accordance with Executive Order 13382. Under that order, entities or individuals designated by the Administration as *"proliferation-supporting"* are subject to sanctions, including impoundment of any U.S.-based assets. U.S. persons are prohibited from conducting any transactions with designated entities. Furthermore, under the Comprehensive Iran Sanctions, Accountability, and Divestment Act of 2010 (CISADA, P.L. 111-195), any foreign bank that conducts transactions with designated entities is subject to being barred from operating in the United States. The Order is not specific to Iran, and hundreds of entities having nothing to do with Iran-related proliferation are designated under the Order. Nevertheless, the effect of these Orders has been unclear, largely because in virtually all cases the entities sanctioned have not had any U.S.-based assets or depended on or entered into transactions with U.S. firms.

The Trump Administration used the Order within days of Iran's January 29 missile test. On February 3, 2017, the Treasury Department designated 17 individuals and entities based in Iran, China, and the Persian Gulf for sanctions under Executive Order 13382. On March 21, 2017, eleven entities were sanctioned under the Iran, North Korea, and Syria Nonproliferation Act, which I discuss further below. A few of them were those sanctioned on February 3 under Executive Order 13382.

Executive Order is 13324, issued a day after the September 11, 2001 terrorist attacks on the United States, imposes the same sanctions as does 13382, but on entities or individuals determined to be *supporting acts of international terrorism*. Executive Order 13224 is also not specific to Iran, and a great many entities designated under that Order are related to Al Qaeda, the Islamic State, and other organizations that Iran does not support. On February 3, under Executive Order 13224, the Treasury Department designated as terrorism-supporting entities eight individuals and companies linked to the IRGC-QF. The Treasury Department action cited the entities as providers of funds and other support to Lebanese Hezbollah and as procurers of aviation spare parts for the IRGC-QF.

Sanctions on the IRGC

A broad range of sanctions are in place in an effort to limit the IRGC's military capabilities as well as the IRGC-QF's regional "malign activities." The JCPOA does not require the United States to cease applying any sanctions on the IRGC, its affiliates, or on entities determined to be conducting transactions with the IRGC or its affiliates.

The IRGC is designated as a proliferation-supporting entity under Executive Order 13382, as an entity that has abused the human rights of Iranian citizens under Executive Order 13553 (same penalties as for 13382). The IRGC's cyber unit has been designated as contributing to the repression of the Iranian people through cyber activities under Executive Order 13606 (same penalties as under the other two Orders). The IRGC-QF is designated as a terrorism-supporting entity under Executive Order 13224; as an entity that has supported Iranian proliferation under the Iran, North Korea, and Syria Nonproliferation Act (see below); and as an entity that has contributed to the repression of the Syrian people under Executive Order 13572 (same penalties as the Orders above). Numerous corporate affiliates and entities assisting the IRGC and IRGC-QF are also designated under these Orders, including technology and weapons suppliers, financial institutions that generate funds or help the IRGC and IRGC-QF move money, air transportation services, trading houses, and many other types of entities. Nevertheless, as was mentioned above, virtually none of these entities has been found to have U.S.-based assets or appreciable U.S.-based business transactions.

U.S. secondary sanctions still apply as well. Under CISADA, which was not required to be waived by the JCPOA, foreign banks that deal with such sanctioned Iranian entities are subject to being barred from the U.S. financial industry. However, in all likelihood, foreign banks that deal with the IRGC or its affiliates

21

neither have nor seek any presence in the United States, meaning that the applicable provision of the CISADA law would likely have little effect. Similarly, the Iran Threat Reduction and Syria Human Rights Act of 2012 (ITRSHA, P.L. 112-158) authorizes the application of sanctions enumerated in the Iran Sanctions Act (P.L. 104-172, as amended) to entities or persons that transact business with the IRGC or its affiliates. ITRSHA also authorizes certain sanctions (a ban on U.S. assistance or credits, on U.S. defense-related exports, or exports of controlled technology) to foreign countries determined to have provided financial or technical support, or goods and services, to members and affiliates of the IRGC.

Foreign Terrorist Organization Designations and the IRGC.[26] The "Anti-Terrorism and Effective Death Penalty Act of 1996 (P.L. 104-132) authorizes sanctions on organizations that the State Department determines:

- engages in, or has engaged in, terrorist activity as designated by the Secretary of State, after consultation with the Secretary of the Treasury, and
- the organization's terrorism activities threaten the security of United States citizens, national security, foreign policy, or the economy of the United States.

Organizations determined to meet those criteria are to be designated as Foreign Terrorist Organizations (FTOs). The sanctions/penalties imposed on an FTO include denial of admission to the United States for its members, a ban on transactions with that organization or its members, and potential prosecution of a U.S.-based person that provides "material support" to the FTO.

Press reports indicate that the Trump Administration is considering designating the IRGC as an FTO.[27] Currently, 61 groups are designated by the State Department as FTOs. None of the designated organizations designated is a duly-constituted armed force of any government, whereas the IRGC is such an official armed force. The government of Iran has been designated as a state sponsor of international terrorism since January 1984, and sanctions imposed on Iran because of that designation apply to components of the Iranian government, including the IRGC.

Designating the IRGC as an FTO could arguably provoke an Iranian diplomatic backlash, with the potential for a violent response against the United States or its personnel in the region or elsewhere, by the IRGC or any group or government to which the IRGC-QF is providing material support. Alternately, Iran's protests of the designation could be limited to diplomatic and rhetorical means. Designating the IRGC as an FTO would not necessarily add much, if any, material pressure on the IRGC that is not already imposed by existing sanctions.

The Iran, North Korea, and Syria Nonproliferation Act (INKSNA) and the Iran-Iraq Arms Non-Proliferation Act

One Iran-related anti-proliferation law that remains in force—and that has been used to try to hinder Iran's development of ballistic missiles—is the Iran, North Korea, and Syria Nonproliferation Act (INKSNA), as amended (P.L. 106-178; 50 U.S.C. 1701 note). This law authorizes, but does not require, the President to impose sanctions on foreign entities or persons that the executive branch has determined, in a mandated report to Congress, has transferred to any of the three countries equipment or material that is restricted for sale by various nonproliferation conventions (Nuclear Suppliers Group, Missile Technology Control Regime, and others). The sanctions remain in effect "for such time as [the president]

---
[26] See also: CRS In Focus IF10613, *Foreign Terrorist Organization (FTO)*, by John W. Rollins.

[27] "Defense, Intelligence Officials Caution White House on Terrorist Designation for Iran's Revolutionary Guard." *Washington Post*, February 8, 2017. https://www.washingtonpost.com/world/national-security/defense-intelligence-officials-caution-white-house-on-terrorist-designation-for-irans-revolutionary-guards/2017/02/08/228a6e4a-ee28-11e6-b4ff-ac2cf509efe5_story.html?utm_term=.cb1c2a7617ac

may determine"—a period that has been determined by successive administrations to be two years, in general conformity with other statutes related to non-proliferation.

The JCPOA does not require any specific sections of the Act to be waived, but the agreement (Section 4.9.1) appears to commit the United States not to impose sanctions on foreign entities that supply goods to the aspects of Iran's nuclear program that are permissible under the JCPOA. The section commits the United States to ease "nuclear proliferation-related" sanctions "under the Iran, North Korea, and Syria Nonproliferation Act on the acquisition of nuclear-related commodities and services for nuclear activities contemplated in the JCPOA, to be consistent with the U.S. approach to other non-nuclear-weapons states under the [Nuclear Nonproliferation Treaty]."

Successive administrations have imposed sanctions on numerous entities under INKSNA. In most cases, the application period has expired. However, several significant entities and individuals remain sanctioned under INKSNA, including several sanctioned on August 28, 2015 and June 28, 2016: the IRGC-QF, IRGC-QF Commander IRGC Maj. Gen. Qasem Soleimani, Lebanese Hezbollah, two Iran-backed Shia militias in Iraq (Asaib Ahl al Haq and Kata'ib Hezbollah), and several Iran-based industrial entities.

Another anti-proliferation law that is country-specific is the Iran-Iraq Arms Non-Proliferation Act of 1992, as amended (Title XVI of P.L. 102-484). That law authorizes sanctions, for a period of two years, on foreign firms or governments that contribute to efforts by Iran (or Iraq) to acquire chemical, biological, or nuclear weapons or "destabilizing numbers and types" of advanced conventional weapons. The law's definition of advanced conventional weapons specifically includes cruise missiles. The JCPOA does not require this law to be waived, and it remains in force. Nevertheless, entities have been sanctioned under this law on only a few occasions, and not since 2003, suggesting that successive administrations might have found other laws or Orders more effective against Iranian proliferation.

Missile Defense

Considering that the Trump Administration has characterized Iran as a significant national security threat, it is possible that the Administration might seek to enhance the missile defense capabilities of U.S. allies in the region. Virtually all U.S. allies in the region possess at least some ballistic missile defense capability, developed or acquired at least in part to defend against Iran's ballistic missile capabilities and ambitions. The United States has long assisted Israel's efforts to establish a multilayered defense with some capability not only of countering Iran's ballistic missile arsenal, but also the rockets and short-range ballistic missiles that Iran supplies to Hezbollah and Hamas. The GCC states have purchased and deployed versions of the U.S.-made Patriot anti-missile system, and some GCC states are upgrading or considering upgrading to the Theater High Altitude Air Defense (THAAD) system. For over a decade, U.S. officials have sought, with mixed results, to persuade the GCC states to develop a coordinated and integrated ballistic missile defense capability. Apparently, each GCC state has been reluctant to forfeit the degree of control of its own systems or procurement plans that might be required to forge a coordinated regional system.

Further, the U.S. Navy maintains regular deployments of ballistic missile defense (BMD)-capable ships in European waters to defend Europe from potential ballistic missile attacks from countries such as Iran. BMD-capable Aegis ships also operate in the Persian Gulf to provide regional defense against potential ballistic missile attacks from Iran.[28]

---

[28] See also: CRS Report RL33745, *Navy Aegis Ballistic Missile Defense (BMD) Program: Background and Issues for Congress,* by Ronald O'Rourke.

Military Options

The actions taken by the Trump Administration in response to Iran's activities to date might not represent the extent of actions the Administration is considering against Iran. President Trump has stated that "all options are open" to respond to Iran's ballistic missile program or malign regional activities. [29] That policy statement is usually interpreted to include the potential for military action. It is a formulation similar to that used by the Obama Administration and by other previous administrations in discussions of Iran policy and potential U.S. options. The Administration has not, to date, publicly specified criteria or circumstances that could potentially trigger military action against Iran. The universe of potential military action against Iran is broad, particularly insofar as any such action could potentially be directed at Iran's regional allies and proxies, and not necessarily at Iran or its forces themselves.

In conclusion, Madame Chairwoman, as I hope my testimony made apparent, the actions of Iran's regime are often difficult to interpret, and not at all easy to counter without potential consequences for the United States and the region.

I appreciate your invitation to testify and I look forward to your questions.

---

[29] President Trump comments on options on Iran. https://www.youtube.com/watch?v=SI17rudxDv6s

Ms. Ros-Lehtinen. Excellent testimony. Thank you, Mr. Katzman.

We have been joined by Mr. Chabot and Ms. Gabbard. So before we move to the witnesses, I wanted to see if they had an opening statement or anything that is on their mind.

Mr. Chabot. Thank you for offering, but I think I will pass at this time.

Ms. Ros-Lehtinen. Thank you. And I know you are on Judiciary that has a markup right now.

Ms. Gabbard? Okay, thank you.

So, Mr. Eisenstadt, you are up. It is still going on. Thank you, sir.

STATEMENT OF MR. MICHAEL EISENSTADT, KAHN FELLOW, DIRECTOR OF MILITARY AND SECURITY STUDIES PROGRAM, THE WASHINGTON INSTITUTE FOR NEAR EAST POLICY

Mr. Eisenstadt. Chairperson Ros-Lehtinen, Ranking Member Deutch, committee members, thank you for inviting me to address your committee today.

As stated by several committee members in their opening statements, Iran has the largest missile force in the Middle East, consisting of thousands of short- and medium-range ballistic missiles and possibly land-attack cruise missiles. Although its missiles are conventionally armed, many could deliver a nuclear weapon if Iran were ever to acquire such a capability in violation of its NPT obligations and JCPOA commitments.

While the recent nuclear accord with Iran will likely defer such a possibility, it did not impose new constraints on Iran's missile program. On the contrary, Security Council Resolution 2231, which gave international legal force to the nuclear accord, loosened them and included provisions for the lifting of these constraints in 8 years, if not sooner.

Missiles and rockets are central to Iran's way of war and that of its proxies. Missiles permit quick, flexible responses during rapidly moving crises. Missile salvos can generate greater cumulative effects on enemy morale and staying power in a shorter period of time than can terrorist attacks. For these reasons, Iran's missile forces are the backbone of its deterrent and warfighting capabilities.

The United States and its regional partners have been investing significant resources in missile defenses in recent decades. However, the continued growth in size and accuracy of Iran's missile force raise concerns that it could saturate and overwhelm missile defenses in the Gulf and Israel.

This problem will only increase with the passage of time. At current production rates, Iran's missile force could more than double in size by the time the major limits imposed by the JCPOA are lifted in the year 2030.

Iran's growing missile force, in tandem with its growing offensive cyber capabilities, will enable it to target the critical infrastructure and missile defenses of our partners with a powerful one-two punch in the physical and virtual domains, while putting American military bases and forces in the region, including our carrier strike groups, at risk.

An Iranian nuclear missile force would be highly destabilizing. Short missile flight times between Iran and Israel, the lack of reliable crisis communication channels, and the impossibility of knowing whether incoming Iranian missiles are conventional or nuclear could spur Israel and any other regional nuclear states that might emerge in the interim to adopt a launch-on-warning posture, undermining the prospect for a stable nuclear deterrent balance in the region.

So what can be done to deal with this threat? Sanctions, to the degree that they complicate Tehran's ability to procure equipment and special materials for its missile program, to include cruise missiles, are helpful and underscore Washington's commitment to addressing the threat. They are an important element of U.S. policy.

Washington should also continue to press allies, partners, and others, especially states that are members of the Missile Technology Control Regime, to tighten enforcement of export controls to prevent Iran from acquiring technology, equipment, and special materials that are essential to its missile program.

The U.S. also needs to further strengthen its deterrent posture. To this end, it should continue to build up coalition missile defenses in the Middle East. After all, Iran's missile force is a problem to which there is a viable solution, albeit an extremely costly one. And it should continue to strengthen the ability of U.S. and partner nations to deliver long-range precision fires and conduct aerial strikes against Iranian missile bases and launchers to attrite Iran's missile forces "left of launch."

These capabilities also ensure that the U.S. and its partners have the ability to respond in kind to Iranian missile strikes.

But the U.S. response must go beyond missiles. The United States needs a comprehensive strategy toward Iran that pushes back against destabilizing Iranian regional activities, strengthens the JCPOA, and deters Iran from building an industrial-scale nuclear infrastructure or attempting a nuclear breakout down the road.

To this end, the United States should respond in a more assertive fashion to Iranian naval harassment in the Gulf, increase efforts to interdict Iranian arms transfers to regional proxies and partners, ramp up support for non-Salafist opposition groups in Syria, and commit to a long term defense partnership with Iraq.

The intent of these steps would be to restore Washington's credibility in Tehran and alter Iran's cost-benefit calculus vis—vis the United States, inducing it to greater caution in areas where the possibility of a conflict with the United States exists.

As for the nuclear deal, it would be a mistake to tear it up. This would isolate the United States, further complicate the reimposition of sanctions should it prove necessary, and provide Iran with a pretext to resume formerly proscribed nuclear activities.

Rather, the U.S. should strictly enforce the JCPOA, try to address its shortcomings, and maximize the productive use of the decade-plus bought by the agreement.

One of the main flaws of U.S. policy toward Iran is that it pursued a time-buying approach, the JCPOA, without a strategy for how to use the time gained. The United States needs to put together such a strategy now by, first, addressing loopholes and shortcomings in the existing nonproliferation and safeguards re-gime; assembling a broad coalition to persuade Iran to forgo its op-tion to build an industrial-scale nuclear infrastructure once JCPOA-mandated restrictions are lifted after 15 years; and per- haps most importantly, leveraging the credibility conferred by its pushback against destabilizing Iranian regional policies to alter Tehran's nuclear risk calculus, thereby bolstering America's ability to deter a future Iranian nuclear breakout.

I look forward to discussing these matters with you. Thank you.

[The prepared statement of Mr. Eisenstadt follows:]

Testing the Limits: Iran's Ballistic Missile Program, Sanctions, and the IRGC

Michael Eisenstadt
Kahn Fellow and Director, Military and Security Studies Program,
The Washington Institute for Near East Policy

Testimony submitted to the House Foreign Affairs Committee
March 29, 2017

Iran has the largest missile force in the Middle East, consisting of thousands of short- and medium-range ballistic missiles, and possibly land-attack cruise missiles.[1] Although its missiles are conventionally armed, many could deliver a nuclear weapon if Iran were to ever acquire such a capability. While the nuclear accord with Iran—the Joint Comprehensive Plan of Action (JCPOA), which was given international legal force by UN Security Council Resolution 2231—will likely defer such an eventuality, it did not impose new constraints on Iran's missile program. On the contrary, UNSCR 2231 loosened them—and included provisions for their lifting in eight years, if not sooner.[2]

At current production rates, Iran's missile force could more than double in size by the time the major limits imposed by the nuclear deal are lifted at the fifteen year mark—in 2030. By then, Iran's growing missile and cyber capabilities could pose major challenges to regional missile defenses, military and critical infrastructure targets, and civilian population centers. This could make preventive action by Israel or the United States, in the event of an attempted Iranian nuclear breakout, much more costly.

Finally, an Iranian nuclear missile force would be highly destabilizing. Short missile flight times between Iran and Israel, the lack of reliable crisis communication channels, and the impossibility of knowing whether incoming Iranian missiles are conventional or nuclear could someday spur Israel—and any additional regional nuclear states that might emerge in the interim—to adopt a launch-on-warning posture, undermining the prospects for a stable nuclear deterrent balance in the region.

DETERRENCE, WARFIGHTING, PROPAGANDA

The Iran-Iraq War (1980–88) convinced Tehran that a strong, capable missile force is critical to the country's security.[3] Missiles played an important role throughout that war, especially during the February–April 1988 "War of the Cities," when Iraq was able to hit Tehran with extended-range missiles for the first time. Iranian morale was devastated: more than a quarter of Tehran's population fled the city, contributing to the leadership's decision to end the war.[4]

Since then, missiles have been central to Iran's "way of war," which emphasizes the need to avoid or deter conventional conflict while advancing an anti–status quo agenda via shaping activities—particularly propaganda, psychological warfare, and proxy operations. Iran's deterrent/warfighting triad rests on its ability to: (1) threaten navigation through the Strait of Hormuz, (2) conduct unilateral and proxy direct action and terrorist attacks on multiple continents, and (3) launch long-range strikes using its own missiles, or by way of long-range rockets and short-range missiles in the hands of proxies such as Hezbollah.[5] Iran's growing cyber capabilities may eventually become a fourth leg of this deterrent/warfighting triad, enabling it to strike at adversaries and to project power globally, instantaneously, and on a sustained basis, in ways it cannot in the physical domain.[6]

Each leg of the triad has distinct advantages and drawbacks. Efforts to close the strait could roil global financial markets but would be a last resort for Iran because nearly all of its imports and oil exports pass through this route. And even a temporary disruption of traffic through the strait would alienate countries in Europe and Asia that depend on Gulf oil. Moreover, Tehran's ability to wage terrorism has atrophied in recent years—as demonstrated by the ill-conceived plan to assassinate the Saudi ambassador to the United States (2011) and a series of bungled attacks on Israeli targets in Asia (2012). Iran cannot be sure that planned terrorist operations will succeed.[7]

Iran can mass missile fires against population centers to undermine enemy morale, though only a small number of its missiles currently have the accuracy to precisely strike military targets or critical infrastructure; these are largely short-range systems such as the Fateh-110 and its derivatives, and perhaps the longer-range Emad. Longer-range systems such as the Qiam, Shahab-3, and Ghadr (see Table 1) could disrupt enemy operations at much greater ranges, though they lack the accuracy to inflict significant damage on military or civilian installations. With increased accuracy, Iran could effectively target military facilities and critical infrastructure, and greatly stress enemy missile defenses—as nearly every incoming missile would pose a threat and would need to be intercepted.[8] Increased accuracy may be important even if Iran eventually acquires nuclear weapons, given that first- and second-generation devices might provide relatively small yields.

Although terrorist attacks afford Iran a degree of standoff and deniability, follow-on attacks might take weeks or months to plan, and could be difficult to implement against an alerted enemy. By contrast, missiles permit quick, flexible responses during rapidly moving crises. Missile salvos can also generate greater cumulative effects on enemy morale and staying power in a shorter period than can terrorist attacks. For these reasons, Iran's missile force constitutes the backbone of its strategic deterrent.

Iranian officials have often discussed their missile force using terms borrowed from classic deterrence theory. Thus, shortly after the first test launch of the Shahab-3 missile in July 1998, then defense minister Ali Shamkhani explained that to bolster Iran's deterrent capability,

> we have prepared ourselves to absorb the first strike so that it inflicts the least damage on us. We have, however, prepared a second strike which can decisively avenge the first one while preventing a third strike against us.[9]

Iran has likewise threatened to respond to an American or Israeli attack on Iran with a "crushing response,"[10] the destruction of the Israeli cities of Tel Aviv and Haifa,[11] and strikes against U.S. bases throughout the region.[12] Missiles would likely play a central role in any major military contingency that Iran is involved in, at least until its still-nascent offensive cyber capabilities mature, at which point cyber may augment missiles as the mainstay of Iran's strategic forces.[13]

Missiles are also ideally suited to Iran's "resistance doctrine," which posits that victory comes through the demoralization of one's enemies by terrorizing their civilians, bleeding their armies, and denying them success on the battlefield.[14] In this regard, the way in which proxies such as Hezbollah and partners such as Hamas used rockets in recent wars with Israel provides a useful template for understanding the role of conventionally armed missiles in Iran's warfighting doctrine.[15] Moreover, as terror weapons, rockets and missiles are equally effective, given that civilians are indifferent to whether they are killed by unguided or guided systems.

Missiles are also Iran's most potent propaganda weapon. They are a central fixture of just about every regime military parade, where they are often dressed with banners calling for "death to America" and for Israel to be "wiped off the map."[16] They are used as symbols of Iran's growing military power and reach, and as symbolic surrogates for the nuclear arsenal it has ostensibly foresworn. (Many observers will subliminally link missiles and nuclear weapons, since missiles are the delivery system of choice of every nuclear weapons state.) For Iran, missiles are a key psychological warfare prop, and play a central role in its emerging doctrine of nuclear ambiguity and possible long-term efforts to create a recessed or "virtual" nuclear deterrent.[17]

Finally, while most nuclear weapons states created missile forces years after testing their first nuclear weapon and joining the "nuclear club" (due to the significant R&D challenges involved in building missiles), Iran will have a sophisticated missile force and infrastructure in place if it eventually abandons its nuclear nonproliferation commitments. Thus, an Iranian nuclear breakout would produce a more rapid and dramatic transformation in its military capabilities than that typically experienced by new nuclear weapons states, potentially exacerbating the conflict-prone tendencies observed in many new proliferators.[18]

IRAN'S MISSILE INVENTORY

As previously noted, Iran has a large, diverse, highly capable missile force consisting of very accurate short-range solid fuel missiles, less accurate but longer-range liquid-fuel Shahab-type missiles, and land-attack cruise missiles. Its short-range ballistic missiles (SRBMs) are for use against near enemies in the Gulf and include the Fateh-110 (with a claimed range of 300 km), Shahab-1 (300 km), Shahab-2 (500 km), Fateh-313 (500 km), Zulfiqar (700 km), and Qiam (800 km). Its medium-range ballistic missiles (MRBMs) are for use against Israel and include the Shahab-3 (1,000 km), Ghadr (1,600 km), and Emad (1,700 km).[19] (See Table 1 and Figure 1) These are believed to be conventionally armed with unitary high-explosive or submunition (cluster) warheads.[20] The aforementioned MRBMs have sufficient excess range to be launched against Israel and the Gulf states from the heart of Iran, where they would be less vulnerable to preemption, and some may have the ability to fly depressed or lofted trajectories, thereby complicating the task of missile defenses.

Iran has also tested a two-stage solid fuel missile, the Sejjil-2, whose range of over 2,000 km would allow it to target southeastern Europe—though it is apparently still not operational.[21] In June 2011, IRGC Aerospace Force commander Brig. Gen. Amir Ali Hajizadeh announced that Iran was capping the range of its missiles at 2,000 km (sufficient to reach Israel but not Western Europe). He stated that "there is no threat from any country to us other than the U.S. and the Zionist regime" and that "the range of our missiles has been designed on the basis of the distance to the Zionist regime and the U.S. bases in the Persian Gulf region." He added that while Iran "possesses the technology...we have no intention to produce such missiles," implicitly eschewing the development of intercontinental ballistic missiles (ICBMs) in a presumed bid to deflect U.S. and European concerns.[22] However, Iranian defense minister Brig. Gen. Hossein Dehqan stated in August 2016 that "we don't have any limit for the range of liquid- or solid-fuel ballistic missiles," apparently indicating the lifting of the previous self-imposed limit.[23] Accordingly, Iran is reported to have recently tested, unsuccessfully, a version of the North Korean BM-25 Musudan intermediate-range ballistic missile (IRBM), which may have a maximum effective range of 2,500 km.[24]

Table 1: SELECT IRANIAN ROCKETS AND MISSILES

This table demonstrates the degree to which Iran's rocket and missile programs reflect a cautious, incremental approach to military innovation and R&D; the result is an operational rocket and missile force built around a small number of base systems and derivatives.

ROCKET/MISSILE	REPORTED RANGE (KM)	FUEL/PROPULSION	COMMENTS
Fajr-3/-5	45/75	Solid	Mid-range rocket—transferred to Hezbollah
Zelzal-1/-2/-3	125/210/300	Solid	Long-range rocket—transferred to Hezbollah
Fateh-110	300	Solid	Missile derived from Zelzal series rockets—Syria's M-600 (a derivative) transferred to Hezbollah
Khalij-e Fars	300	Solid	Electro-optically guided antiship ballistic missile derived from Fateh-110
Hormuz-1/-2	300	Solid	Antiradiation/antiship missiles—derived from Fateh-110
Shahab-1	300	Liquid	Derived from Russian Scud-B missile via North Korea
Shahab-2	500	Liquid	Derived from Russian Scud-C missile via North Korea
Fateh-313	600	Solid	Extended-range Fateh-110
Zulfiqar	700	Solid	Extended-range Fateh-313
Qiam	800	Liquid	Finless design derived from Shahab-2 missile
Shahab-3	1,000	Liquid	Derived from North Korean Nodong missile
Ghadr	1,600	Liquid	Derived from Shahab-3 missile
Emad	1,700	Liquid	Derived from Ghadr missile, reportedly has a maneuvering RV
Sejjil-2	2,000+	Solid	Multistage missile, test flown but not operational
BM-25	4,000	Liquid	North Korean design based on Russian R-27 submarine-launched ballistic missile, test flown?
Ya Ali	700	Turbojet	Air-launched land-attack cruise missile, operational status unknown
Soumar	2,500–3,000	Turbofan	Ground-launched land-attack cruise missile based on Russian Kh-55?

Sources: Michael Elleman, *Iran's Ballistic Missile Capabilities: A Net Assessment*, IISS Strategic Dossier (London: International Institute for Strategic Studies, 2010); Michael Elleman, "Are Iran's Missiles a Threat?" The Iran Primer (United States Institute of Peace, April 25, 2016), http://iranprimer.usip.org/blog/2016/may/23/part-i-are-iran%E2%80%99s-missiles-threat; Uzi Rubin, *The Global Reach of Iran's Ballistic Missiles*, Memorandum 86 (Tel Aviv: Institute for National Security Studies, 2006), http://www.inss.org.il/uploadimages/import/(FILE)1883302022.pdf; Uzi Rubin, "Rockets and Missiles in the Middle East: Global Implications," PowerPoint presentations, March 2014 and April 2016, http://documents.mx/news-politics/uzi-rubin-global-threat-evolution-an-update.html, and https://rusi.org/sites/default/files/uzi_rubin.pdf; Tal Inbar, "The Ballistic Axis: DPRK and Iran's Cooperation in Missiles and Space—Strategic Implications," PowerPoint presentation, April 21, 2016, http://www.slideshare.net/TWIPubs/the-ballistic-axis-strategic-implications-of-dprk-and-irans-cooperation-in-missiles-and-space.

TWIPubs/the-ballistic-axis-strategic-implications-of-dprk-and-irans-cooperation-in-missiles-and-space.

Iran's Safir space launch vehicle (SLV), which has put four satellites into orbit since 2009, could provide the experience and know-how needed to build an ICBM. Some assessments suggest that the Safir struggled to put a very small satellite into low-earth orbit and has therefore probably reached the outer limits of its performance envelope—and could not serve as an ICBM.[25] In 2010, Iran displayed a full-size mockup of a larger two-stage SLV, the Simorgh, which it first tested in April 2016.[26] It would seem that Iran is keeping its options open for developing an ICBM.[27] Indeed, U.S. intelligence reports indicate that Iran and North Korea are collaborating on the development of a large rocket motor suitable for use in an SLV or ICBM—which may have been the engine tested by North Korea in September 2016 and again in March 2017.[28]

Tehran has also claimed an antiship ballistic missile capability for potential use against U.S. carrier strike groups: the Khalij-e Fars electro-optically guided missile, and its derivatives, the Hormuz-1 antiradiation missile and Hormuz-2 active radar homing missile, each with a claimed range of 300 km. It is not clear that these systems are yet sufficiently accurate or effective to pose a serious threat to U.S. naval surface elements in the Gulf.[29]

As for land-attack cruise missiles, Iran claims to have produced two: the 700-km range air-launched Ya Ali, and the 2,500–3,000 km range ground launched Soumar—which appears to be based on the Russian Raduga Kh-55 missiles obtained some years ago from Ukraine.[30] The Kh-55 was the Soviet air force's primary nuclear-delivery system. It is not clear that either system is operational.

Iran also fields a very large number of rocket systems used by allies, such as Hezbollah, for strategic bombardment. These include the Fajr-3 and 5 (with claimed ranges of 45 and 75 km) and the Zelzal-3 (300 km). During the Iran-Iraq War, rockets played a major role in bombarding Iraqi cities along the border, and they are central to the "way of war" of Hezbollah and Hamas.

Hezbollah is believed to have received relatively small numbers of M-600, SS-21, and Scud-type SRBMs from Syrian stocks, and up to 150,000 short-range rockets from Syria and Iran. In a future war with Israel, Hezbollah could use its highly accurate M-600 missiles (Syrian versions of the Iranian Fateh-110) to hit strategic targets—e.g., military headquarters in Tel Aviv, power stations, Israel's offshore natural gas production facilities, Ben Gurion International Airport, and its nuclear reactor at Dimona—and could attempt to suppress Israeli missile defenses with massive rocket and missile salvos from Lebanon to facilitate the penetration of its own SRBMs, or MRBMs launched by Iran.

While many of Iran's missiles are mounted on mobile launchers (some of which are configured to look like civilian vehicles), others are deployed in large numbers of austere "onetime-use" silos[31] and massive underground launch complexes.[32] These launch complexes consist of tunnel systems that service underground missile halls built under mountains as well as pre-surveyed launch sites adjacent to these mountains. Most of Iran's silo fields and launch complexes are located in the country's northwest, toward the frontier with Iraq, and in the vicinity of the Persian Gulf.[33] The use of mobile launchers and underground facilities would greatly complicate preventive or preemptive targeting of its missile force. It would enable Iran to undertake prolonged pre-launch preparations for liquid-fuel missiles and to conduct mass fires from protected positions without fear of interdiction or disruption by the enemy. The use of underground facilities could also shield preparations for a surprise strike.[34]

Iran will likely continue producing SRBMs and MRBMs and may introduce IRBMs in the coming years. UNSCR Resolution 2231, which "called upon [Iran] not to undertake any activity related to ballistic missiles designed to be capable of delivering nuclear weapon," has not proved a hindrance in this regard, and at any rate, Iran has pledged to ignore it.[35] Assuming Iran continues its current production rate of fifty-plus MRBMs a year,[36] in fifteen to twenty years, when most of the restrictions imposed by the nuclear accord are lifted, it will have more than doubled its missile inventory. This will further stress regional missile defenses and dramatically increase the potential weight of Iranian missile strikes in a future conflict.

The United States and its Israeli and Gulf Arab allies have been investing significant resources in missile defense in recent decades—while Israel has been investing in rocket defenses as well. America and its Gulf partners, however, still face major challenges: insufficient numbers of interceptors to deal with Iranian saturation tactics, gaps in the coverage of currently deployed missile defenses, and the lack of an integrated missile defense architecture in the Gulf.[37] The continued growth in size and accuracy of Iran's missile force ensures its ability to saturate and overwhelm missile defenses in the Gulf and Israel. Moreover, the improving accuracy of its missile force, in tandem with its growing offensive cyber capabilities, will enable it to target enemy critical infrastructure and missile defenses with a powerful one-two punch in the physical and virtual domains. This will likely render an American or Israeli preventive strike much more costly, and hence less likely, should Iran attempt a nuclear breakout.

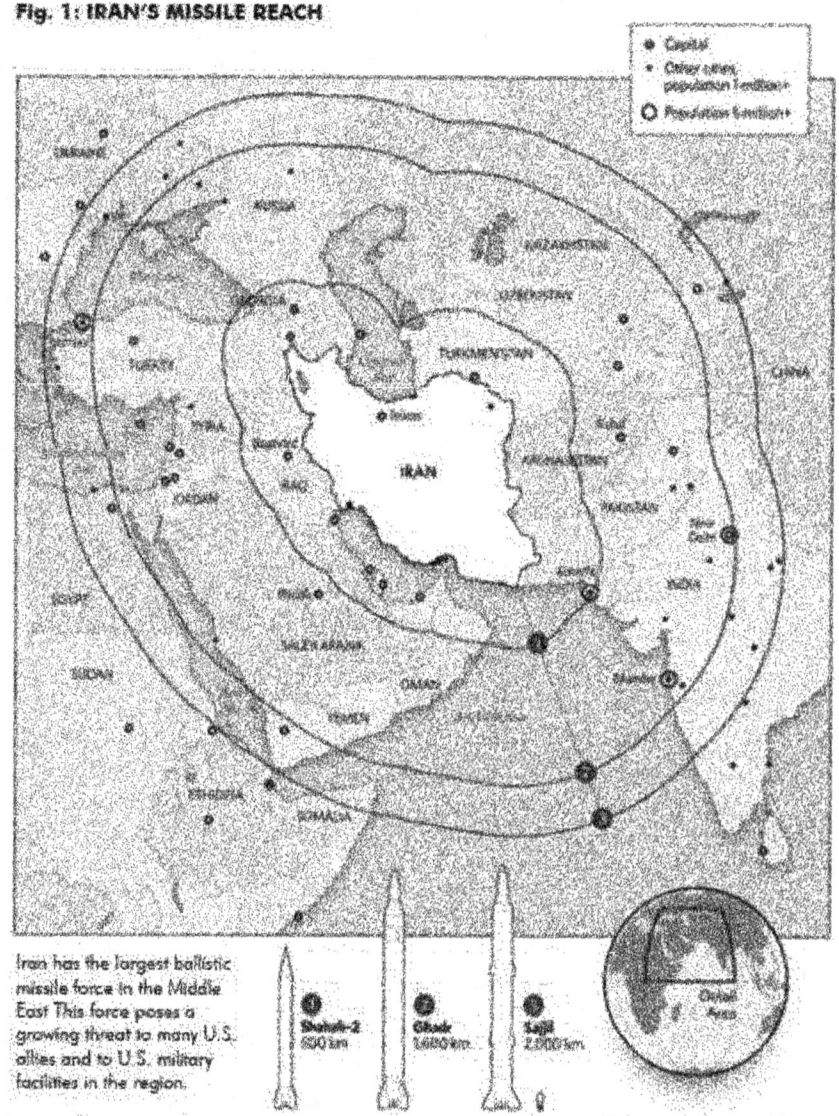

Fig. 1: IRAN'S MISSILE REACH

Iran has the largest ballistic missile force in the Middle East. This force poses a growing threat to many U.S. allies and to U.S. military facilities in the region.

Source: International Institute for Strategic Studies, *The Military Balance 2014* (London: Routledge, 2014). heritage.org

NUCLEAR LINKAGES—POLICY IMPLICATIONS

The International Atomic Energy Agency's "final assessment" of outstanding issues regarding Iran's nuclear program, published in December 2015, confirmed the existence of a number of activities dating to 2002-3 "related to the development of a nuclear payload for a missile," including the integration of a spherical payload (presumably a nuclear implosion device) into a

Shahab-3 reentry vehicle (RV) and a fusing, arming, and firing system for the spherical payload to ensure it remained safe until the RV reached its designated target.[38]

Moreover, in 2004, Iran began deploying triconic, or "baby bottle," RVs—a design almost exclusively associated with nuclear-armed missiles—on its Shahab variants (e.g., the Qiam and Ghadr). Some analysts believe that Iran may have deployed the triconic RV to enhance the accuracy of its conventional warheads and achieve higher terminal velocities to defeat missile defenses.[39] But Iran's experience in designing, testing, and operating triconic RVs could also expedite deployment of a miniaturized nuclear device. The discovery that members of the A. Q. Khan nuclear smuggling network possessed plans for smaller, more advanced nuclear weapon designs that might have found their way to Iran, have strengthened these concerns.[40]

As mentioned previously, the ability to place a first generation nuclear device atop a missile—an achievement that took a decade for most nuclear weapons states—could magnify the destabilizing impact of an Iranian nuclear breakout. Moreover, short flight times and the absence of crisis hotlines might cause Israel—and any other regional nuclear states that emerge in the interim—to eventually respond to an Iranian nuclear breakout by adopting nuclear force postures that include launch-on-warning or pre-delegation of missile launch authority to military commanders. Such measures could increase the risks of accidental or unauthorized use of nuclear weapons.[41] These potential outcomes may increase the incentive for prevention or proliferation by regional states able to do so.

Iran's creation of a hybrid missile force capable of delivering conventional or nuclear warheads would add another destabilizing element to the mix. In a crisis or war, for instance, Israel might not be able to discern whether incoming Iranian missiles are conventional or nuclear, confronting it with the dilemma of absorbing what might be a devastating nuclear first strike—as some missiles will almost certainly get through its defenses—or launching a nuclear counterstrike in response to what might be a conventional attack.[42] In such circumstances, Israel's nuclear forces might be kept on hair-trigger alert. Reckless Iranian rhetoric, moreover, including ritual calls for Israel's destruction, might incline Israeli decisionmakers to interpret Iranian actions in the darkest possible light.[43]

Israel's missile defenses reduce the risk posed by this scenario by ensuring the survival of the country's nuclear second-strike capability[44] (consisting of strike aircraft, and land- and sea-based missiles) and its ability to unleash a devastating counterstrike against Iran.[45] But should Iran continue to build large numbers of increasingly accurate missiles and start employing penetration aids and countermeasures (simple decoys, a modest terminal-phase maneuver capability, chaff, or low-power electronic countermeasures), the efficacy of Israel's missile defenses could come into question, with negative implications for its margin of security and the potential for miscalculation during a crisis.[46] Risk, however, cuts both ways, and Tehran has to consider the potential for such a catastrophic miscalculation, which could jeopardize Iran's very survival. This should be a major theme of Washington's quiet and public diplomacy to shape the Islamic Republic's future nuclear choices.

Finally, while there is no evidence that Iran's leaders adhere to a "messianic, apocalyptic" ideology or that they view mutual assured destruction as "an inducement" and "not a constraint," in the words of Middle East historian Bernard Lewis,[47] neither should much credence be given to facile claims that because deterrence worked during the Cold War, it would also work with Iran.[48] Such claims are based on a superficial and selective reading of the Islamic Republic's strategic conduct.[49] For while Iran's leadership has shown that it is "rational" and generally risk averse, it is also occasionally prone to reckless behavior and to overreach—tendencies that its grandiose ambitions tend to amplify. (Examples of such behavior include the Beirut Marine barracks bombing in 1983, the Khobar Towers bombing in 1996, and the plot to assassinate the Saudi ambassador to the United States in 2011.)[50]

Indeed, Tehran's resistance doctrine raises the possibility that under certain circumstances, Iranian decisionmakers might follow a path that could inadvertently lead to a conflict with Israel or the United States, or that they might welcome a limited conflict to achieve certain policy objectives.[51] Indeed, the resistance doctrine has already propelled Hezbollah and Hamas into four destructive wars with Israel (one involving Hezbollah, three involving Hamas). And Iran has responded to its perceived "victory" in its nuclear negotiations by testing to see what kinds of activities it can get away with without jeopardizing sanctions relief and foreign investment. Thus, it has continued with the covert procurement of technology for its missile programs,[52] engaged in aggressive behavior in the Persian Gulf,[53] increased the pace of missile tests and exercises in defiance of UNSCR 2231 (holding one missile launch "event" in the 20 months prior to the announcement of the interim Joint Plan of Action in November 2013, one missile launch event in the 20 months during which the JCPOA was negotiated, and eight missile launch events in the 20 months since the conclusion of the JCPOA in July 2015),[54] and transferred arms to proxies and allies in Syria, Iraq, and Yemen,[55] in violation of the spirit, if not the letter, of the nuclear accord and UN Security Council Resolution 2231.

Table 2: Iranian Missile Launch Events by Year

Year	Count	
1998	2	
1999	0	
2000	2	
2001	0	
2002	2	
2003	1	
2004	2	
2005	0	
2006	4	
2007	1	
2008	3	
2009	4	
2010	1	
2011	3	
2012	1	
2013	0	
2014	1	
2015	2	
2016	5	
2017	1	(includes only the first three months of the year)

Methodology: This table tallies the number of days in which *publicized* MRBM tests or launches occurred, and may include individual or multiple launches on the same day. MRBMs include the Shahab-3 and its variants (Qiam, Ghadr, and Emad) and the Sejjil. It is worth noting that Iran publicized one missile launch event in the 20 months prior to the announcement of the interim Joint Plan of Action in November 2013, one launch event in the 20 months during which the JCPOA was negotiated, and eight launch events in the 20 months since the conclusion of the JCPOA in July 2015.

Sources: Greg Thielmann, *Iranian Missiles and the Comprehensive Nuclear Deal*, Arms Control Association Iran Nuclear Brief, May 7, 2014, https://www.armscontrol.org/files/Iran_Brief_Iranian_Missiles_Comprehensive_Nuclear_Deal.pdf; Behnam Ben Taleblu, *Iranian Ballistic Missile Tests Since the Nuclear Deal*, Foundation for Defense of Democracies, February 9, 2017, http://www.defenddemocracy.org/content/uploads/documents/20917_Behnam_Ballistic_Missile.pdf; Iranian and foreign media.

A country's leaders do not have to be irrational to take irresponsible risks with potentially catastrophic consequences. By reducing the margin of error for regional decisionmakers, Iran's growing missile force could increase the potential for miscalculation and complicate efforts to create a stable deterrent balance with a potential nuclear Iran. The failure to effectively address Iran's missile program was therefore a major shortcoming of the nuclear deal and Security Resolution 2231. Iran's missile program should be an integral part of any future efforts to renegotiate aspects of the nuclear deal[56] in order to rectify its shortcomings and defuse a potential crisis should the Islamic Republic: (1) withdraw from the JCPOA because its high expectations were not met; (2) restart clandestine nuclear activities in the JCPOA's out-years, when many of its intrusive monitoring provisions disappear; or (3) opt to build an industrial-scale nuclear infrastructure, as permitted by the JCPOA, once limits on the size of its program are lifted fifteen years from now, potentially reducing its breakout time to a matter of weeks.[57]

In the meantime, Washington should do what it can to strengthen the enforcement of export controls by allies, partners, and others—especially states that have joined the Missile Technology Control Regime (MTCR)—to prevent Iran from acquiring equipment and special materials needed for its missile program. It should likewise do what it can to devalue the utility of the missile component of Tehran's deterrence/warfighting triad, into which Iran has invested billions of dollars and massive human and material resources, by strengthening America's ability to deter by denial, as well as punishment.[58] Thus, the United States should continue to build up coalition missile defenses and efforts to create an integrated missile defense architecture in the Middle East; after all, Iran's missile force is a problem to which there is a viable solution—albeit an extremely costly one. It should also continue to strengthen U.S. and partner nation forces capable of delivering long-range precision fires and conducting aerial strikes against Iranian missile bases and launchers, to attrite Iran's missile force on the ground and thereby reduce the burden on coalition missile defenses.[59] These forces also provide the United States and its partners with an ability to respond in-kind to Iranian missiles strikes, should they desire to do so.

Finally, the United States should ensure that coalition missile defenses are hardened against cyberattacks by Iran and its proxies. It should encourage its Gulf Arab partners to improve their civil defenses (Israel's capabilities in this area are already fairly robust). And it should counter Iranian missile propaganda and psychological warfare with a strategic communication campaign that highlights the extremely capable missile defenses of the United States and its allies, and emphasizes that Iranian missiles strikes would prompt an overwhelming response in-kind by coalition air and missile forces.

BEYOND MISSILES: THE NEED FOR A COMPREHENSIVE IRAN STRATEGY

The U.S. response to Iran's growing missile capabilities needs to be nested in a comprehensive policy toward Iran that pushes back against destabilizing Iranian regional activities, strengthens the JCPOA, and in the long run—deters Iran from building an industrial scale nuclear infrastructure or attempting a nuclear breakout. To succeed in all these areas, however, the United States needs to restore American credibility. Iran has learned that it can seize embassies and violate other diplomatic norms, wage proxy warfare against the United States and other enemies, and violate its non-proliferation commitments by building covert nuclear facilities, without incurring excessive risk of a military response. To reverse this trend, the U.S. must demonstrate—by word and deed—that it is no longer willing to accept what it accepted in the past. To this end, it should push back against destabilizing Iranian activities by:

- Responding in a more assertive fashion to Iranian harassment of U.S. naval forces in the Persian Gulf;[60]

- Interdicting more vigorously Iranian arms transfers to its partners and proxies and supporting the activities of allies (such as Israel and the UAE) engaged in such activities;[61]

- Ramping-up support for non-Salafist rebel groups in Syria (but only after the defeat of Islamic State forces in Iraq, so as not to complicate the counter-IS campaign there). Support for non-Salafist opposition groups might help consolidate cease-fires in some places and reduce refugee flows from these areas. And it could impose costs on the Assad regime and its allies (Hezbollah, Iran, and its Shiite foreign legions) in areas where the former are not observing a ceasefire, potentially miring them in an open-ended conflict that could limit their troublemaking potential elsewhere in the region;

- Committing to a long-term security assistance relationship with Iraq to counter Iranian influence there, prevent Iraq from becoming an Iranian client state, and complicate Iranian efforts to build a land bridge to the Levant.[62]

The intent of these measures would be to alter Tehran's cost/benefit calculus vis-à-vis Washington and induce greater caution on its part in areas where the possibility of a conflict with the United States exists.

As for the nuclear deal, it would be a mistake to tear it up; this would isolate the United States, further complicate the re-imposition of sanctions should it prove necessary, and provide Iran with a pretext to resume formerly proscribed nuclear activities. Rather, the U.S. should strictly enforce the JCPOA, try to redress its shortcomings, and maximize the productive use of the decade-plus bought by the agreement. One of the main flaws of U.S. policy toward Iran is that it pursued a time-buying agreement—the JCPOA—without a strategy for how to use the time gained. The United States needs to put together such as strategy now.

To redress the JCPOA's most critical shortcomings, Washington might consider a bilateral "more for more" agreement with Tehran in which the U.S. would agree to go beyond what is required of it by the JCPOA with respect, for instance, to encouraging investment in Iran, if Iran would agree to go beyond what is required of it by the JCPOA. These could include, inter alia, Iran accepting constraints on centrifuge R&D and production as well as missile R&D and testing, and forgoing its option for an industrial-scale nuclear infrastructure. Such a bilateral agreement would not require amendment of the JCPOA or the assent of the other members of the EU3+3. The main drawback of such an agreement is that it could provide Iran with economic benefits that would enable it to intensify its destabilizing regional activities, and to build up its conventional military.

However, it is hard to believe that Iran would agree to new limits on its nuclear and missile programs now that the most onerous sanctions on it have been lifted. In fact, there are no signs that Tehran is interested in a "more for more" agreement with the United States at this time—particularly one that would require it to accept constraints on its centrifuge R&D and missile programs, or forego the option of an industrial-scale nuclear program. Nor is it clear that the benefits to Washington of a "more for more" agreement would offset the costs—especially since Washington would have to pay up-front for a commitment by Tehran to forego its option to build an industrial scale nuclear infrastructure, which the Islamic Republic could always renege on at a later date, after having pocketed economic benefits for more than a decade. (It is not clear that Iran is committed to such a course of action anyhow, and its intentions in this regard may not become clear for years to come.) Still, as long is Tehran continues to complain about the terms of the nuclear agreement, the possibilities offered by a "more for more" deal in all its various permutations, should be examined.

Finally, the U.S. should use the time gained by the JCPOA to act along four lines of effort. Specifically, it should:

- Address loopholes and shortcomings in the existing nuclear non-proliferation and safeguards regime (to include the Additional Protocol, which will remain in effect indefinitely once the monitoring arrangements established by the JCPOA are lifted after 15-25 years), and seek support for applying some of the innovative aspects of the JCPOA more broadly, in other countries, so that Iran may be encouraged to abide by key aspects of the agreement indefinitely;[63]

- Assemble a broad coalition to convince Iran to forego its option under the JCPOA to build an industrial-scale nuclear infrastructure once restrictions on its program are lifted after 15 years. In particular, it should work with countries that have a vested interest (economic or otherwise) in Tehran not developing an independent fuel cycle (such as Russia, which is Iran's main supplier of reactor fuel) to discourage, or at least not abet such a development;

- Launch a long-term information campaign to convince both the people and the regime of the dangers of nuclear fuel cycle facilities such as nuclear reactors, in the event of a major earthquake (nearly all of Iran is an active seismic zone) or in wartime—when they may be targeted by terrorists or neighboring states;[64]

- Leverage the credibility conferred by its pushback against destabilizing Iranian regional policies to bolster deterrence vis-à-vis an Iranian nuclear breakout, emphasizing that traditional intelligence methods and novel cyber capabilities ensure that the United States will almost certainly detect an attempted Iranian nuclear breakout, and that it will use all means at its disposal to prevent such an eventuality.[65]

To support this last line of effort and preserve its options for dealing with future nuclear proliferators, the United States should continue work on conventional penetrator munitions and other capabilities that will be necessary to deal with the hardened, deeply buried targets of the future.[66]

---

[1] This testimony is an updated and abridged version of the author's publication *The Role of Missiles in Iran's Military Strategy*, Washington Institute for Near East Policy, Research Note No. 39, November 2016, http://www.washingtoninstitute.org/uploads/Documents/pubs/ResearchNote39-Eisenstadt.pdf.

[2] UN Security Council Resolution 2231, S/RES/2231 (2015), July 20, 2015, http://www.un.org/en/ga/search/view_doc.asp?symbol=S/RES/2231(2015). See also Uzi Rubin, "The Nuclear Agreement Boosts Iran's Missile Threat," Defense News, October 5, 2015, http://www.defensenews.com/story/defense/commentary/2015/10/05/nuclear-agreement-boosts-irans-missile-threat/73388484/.

[3] Farzin Nadimi, "Iran Seeks to Strengthen Its Deterrence by Showing Off Its Missile Force," *PolicyWatch* 2512 (Washington Institute for Near East Policy, October 28, 2015), http://www.washingtoninstitute.org/policy-analysis/view/iran-seeks-to-strengthen-its-deterrence-by-showing-off-its-missile-force.

[4] Warren Richey, "Iranians Await Iraqi Attacks in Campgrounds and Luxury Hotels," *Christian Science Monitor*, April 15, 1988, p. 11.

[5] Michael Eisenstadt, *The Strategic Culture of the Islamic Republic of Iran: Religion, Expediency, and Soft Power in an Era of Disruptive Change*, Middle East Studies Monograph 7 (Marine Corps University, November 2015), pp. 8–9, http://www.washingtoninstitute.org/uploads/Documents/pubs/MESM_7_Eisenstadt.pdf.

[6] Michael Eisenstadt, *Iran's Lengthening Cyber Shadow*, Research Note 34 (Washington DC: Washington Institute, 2016), http://www.washingtoninstitute.org/uploads/Documents/pubs/ResearchNote34_Eisenstadt.pdf.

[7] Matthew Levitt, *Hizballah and the Qods Force in Iran's Shadow War with the West*, Policy Focus 123 (Washington DC: Washington Institute, 2013), http://www.washingtoninstitute.org/uploads/Documents/pubs/PolicyFocus123.pdf.

[8] Regarding the limitations of Iran's missile force, see Jacob L. Heim, "The Iranian Missile Threat to Air Bases," *Air & Space Power Journal* (July/August 2015): pp. 27–49, http://www.au.af.mil/au/afri/aspj/digital/pdf/articles/2015-JulAug/F-Heim.pdf; Joshua R. Itzkowitz Shifrinson and Miranda Priebe, "A Crude Threat: The Limits of an Iranian Missile Campaign against Saudi Arabian Oil," *International Security* 36, no. 1 (Summer 2011): pp. 167–201, http://hdl.handle.net/1721.1/66242. The growing accuracy of Iran's missile forces will eventually render these assessments obsolete.

[9] "Defence Minister Comments on Production of Shahab-3 Missile," Vision of the Islamic Republic of Iran Network 2, Tehran, July 30, 1998, translated in BBC Monitoring Summary of World Broadcasts, August 3, 1998.

[10] Fars News Agency, "Deputy Top Commander: Crushing Response Waiting for U.S. Military Threats against Iran," July 3, 2015, http://english.farsnews.com/newstext.aspx?nn=13940412000454.

[11] Marcus George and Zahra Hosseinian, "Iran Will Destroy Israeli Cities if Attacked: Khamenei," Reuters, March 21, 2013, http://www.reuters.com/article/2013/03/21/us-iran-khamenei-idUSBRE92K0LA20130321; Fars News Agency, "Iranian Top Commander: Zionists' Attack against Iran Ends in Razing Israel," July 10, 2015, http://english.farsnews.com/newstext.aspx?nn=13940419000998 .

[12] Fars News Agency, "Commander: IRGC Will Destroy 35 U.S. Bases in Region if Attacked," July 4, 2012, http://english2.farsnews.com/newstext.php?nn=9103084990.

[13] Eisenstadt, *Iran's Lengthening Cyber Shadow*, http://www.washingtoninstitute.org/uploads/Documents/pubs/ResearchNote34_Eisenstadt.pdf.

[14] Eisenstadt, *The Strategic Culture of the Islamic Republic of Iran*, http://www.washingtoninstitute.org/uploads/Documents/pubs/MESM_7_Eisenstadt.pdf.

[15] Uzi Rubin, "Palestinian Rockets versus Israeli Missiles in the Second Gaza War," *PolicyWatch* 2011 (Washington Institute for Near East Policy, December 21, 2012), http://www.washingtoninstitute.org/policy-analysis/view/rockets-versus-missiles-in-the-second-gaza-war.

[16] Mary Jordan and Karl Vick, "World Leaders Condemn Iranian's Call to Wipe Israel 'Off the Map,'" *Washington Post*, October 28, 2005, http://www.washingtonpost.com/wp-dyn/content/article/2005/10/27/AR2005102702221.html.

[17] Michael Eisenstadt, *What Iran's Chemical Past Tells Us about Its Nuclear Future*, Research Note 17 (Washington DC: Washington Institute, 2014), pp. 1, 8, 13–14, https://www.washingtoninstitute.org/uploads/Documents/pubs/ResearchNote17_Eisenstadt2.pdf.

[18] Michael Horowitz, "The Spread of Nuclear Weapons and International Conflict: Does Experience Matter?" *Journal of Conflict Resolution* 53, no. 2 (April 2009): 234–57, http://belfercenter.hks.harvard.edu/files/uploads/Horowitz_The_Spread_of_Nuclear_Weapons.pdf.

[19] Uzi Rubin, presentation before the Missile Defense Advocacy Alliance, September 11, 2015, http://missiledefenseadvocacy.org/alert/the-good-the-bad-and-the-ugly-going-forward-no-matter-your-assessment-of-the-iran-nuclear-dealmissile-defense-continues-to-be-vital-to-gulf-security/.

[20] Michael Elleman, *Iran's Ballistic Missile Capabilities: A Net Assessment*, IISS Strategic Dossier (London: International Institute for Strategic Studies, 2010), pp. 121–25.

[21] Tal Inbar, "The Ballistic Axis: DPRK and Iran's Cooperation in Missiles and Space—Strategic Implications," April 21, 2016, http://www.slideshare.net/TWIPubs/the-ballistic-axis-strategic-implications-of-dprk-and-irans-cooperation-inmissiles-and-space.

[22] Associated Press, "Iran 'Will Not Make Longer-Range Missiles as Israel Is Already in Reach,'" *Guardian*, June 28, 2011, https://www.theguardian.com/world/2011/jun/28/iran-longer-range-missiles-israel. Likewise, in a December 2012 news conference, IRGC Aerospace Force commander Brig. Gen. Amir Ali Hajizadeh stated that "we don't need missiles with over 2,000 km but we have the technology to build them," adding that "Israel is our longest-range target." Fars News Agency, "Commander Names Israel as Iran's Long-Range Target," December 10, 2012, http://english2.farsnews.com/newstext.php?nn=9107125969 And in a December 2013 speech, IRGC commander Maj. Gen. Mohammad Ali Jafari stated, "We are still now increasing the range of our missiles, but currently the Supreme Leader has commanded that we limit the range of our missiles to 2,000 km." Will Fulton and Amir Toumaj, "Iran News Round Up," December 11, 2013, http://www.irantracker.org/iran-news-round-december-11-2013.

[23] Fars News Agency, "DM: Iran's Ballistic Missile Development Program Not Confined to Any Range," August 27, 2016, http://en.farsnews.com/newstext.aspx?nn=13950606000599.

[24] Lucas Tomlinson, "Iran Conducts 4th Missile Test since Signing Nuke Deal," FoxNews.com, July 15, 2016, http://www.foxnews.com/world/2016/07/15/exclusive-iran-conducts-4th-missile-test-since-signing-nuke-deal.html. For more on the Musudan, see Ralph Savelsberg and James Kiessling, "North Korea's Musudan Missile: A Performance Assessment," *38 North*, December 20, 2016, http://38north.org/2016/12/musudan122016/.

[25] Elleman, *Iran's Ballistic Missile Capabilities*, pp. 26–32. See also Uzi Rubin, "Showcase of Missile Proliferation: Iran's Missile and Space Program," *Arms Control Today* 42, no. 1 (January/February 2012), pp. 14–20, https://www.armscontrol.org/act/2012_01-02/Showcase_of_Missile_Proliferation_Irans_Missile_and_Space_Program.

[26] Tamir Eshel, "Simorgh First Launch—An Iranian Success or Failure?" *Defense Update*, April 24, 2016, http://defenseupdate.com/20160424_simorgh.html.

[27] Farzin Nadimi, *Iran's Missile Arsenal and the Nuclear Negotiations*, Policy Note 22 (Washington DC: Washington Institute, 2014), p. 2, http://www.washingtoninstitute.org/uploads/Documents/pubs/PolicyNote22_Nadimi4.pdf.

[28] John Schilling, "A New Engine for a New Satellite Launch Vehicle?" *38 North*, March 20, 2017, http://38north.org/2017/03/jschilling032017/; U.S. Department of the Treasury, "Treasury Sanctions Those Involved in Ballistic Missile Procurement for Iran," press release, January 17, 2016, https://www.treasury.gov/press-center/press-releases/Pages/jl0322.aspx; David E. Sanger and William J. Broad, "To the Moon, North Korea? Or Does a Rocket Have a Darker Aim?" *New York Times*, September 26, 2016, http://www.nytimes.com/2016/09/27/world/asia/north-korea-rocket-moon.html. For more background on this, see Michael Elleman, "North Korea–Iran Missile Cooperation," *38 North*, September 22, 2016, http://38north.org/2016/09/melleman092216/.

[29] Michael Elleman, personal correspondence with author, October 18, 2012.

[30] Inbar, "The Ballistic Axis," http://www.slideshare.net/TWIPubs/the-ballistic-axis-strategic-implications-of-dprk-andirans-cooperation-in-missiles-and-space.

[31] These silos are much larger than needed for Iran's current missiles, and may have been built to accommodate larger missiles in the future. Rubin, "Showcase of Missile Proliferation," https://www.armscontrol.org/act/2012_01-02/Showcase_of_Missile_Proliferation_Irans_Missile_and_Space_Program.

[32] For videos of Iranian missile launchers disguised as civilian vehicles, see seconds 6–16 of this YouTube video, "Iran underground tunnel of mobile missiles...," 1:48, November 27, 2014, https://www.youtube.com/watch?v=TjNEU58xrOQ.

[33] Nadimi, "Iran Seeks to Strengthen Its Deterrence," http://www.washingtoninstitute.org/policy-analysis/view/iran-seeksto-strengthen-its-deterrence-by-showing-off-its-missile-force. See also William Broad, "Iran Unveils Missile Silos as It Begins War Games," *New York Times*, June 24, 2011, http://www.nytimes.com/2011/06/28/world/middleeast/28iran.html?_r=0 .

[34] Inbar, "The Ballistic Axis," http://www.slideshare.net/TWIPubs/the-ballistic-axis-strategic-implications-of-dprk-andirans-cooperation-in-missiles-and-space.

[35] Bozorgmehr Sharafedin, "Iran Says It Will Not Accept Any Restrictions on Missile Program," Reuters, December 16, 2015, http://www.reuters.com/article/us-iran-military-missiles-idUSKBN0TZ2DC20151216.

[36] Uzi Rubin, personal correspondence, December 21, 2012.

[37] Michael Eisenstadt, "Missile Defense and the Islamic Republic of Iran: Contribution to Deterrence, Defense, and Crisis Stability," presentation to the Fisher Institute for Air and Space Strategic Studies, December 17, 2014, http://www.fisher.org.il/2014/IranMissileDefense.pdf .

[38] International Atomic Energy Agency, "Final Assessment on Past and Present Outstanding Issues regarding Iran's Nuclear Programme," December 2, 2015, GOV/2015/68, https://www.iaea.org/sites/default/files/gov-2015-68.pdf.

[39] "Wisconsin Project Interview with Uzi Rubin on Iran's Missile Program," Iran Watch, September 17, 2009, http://www.iranwatch.org/our-publications/interview/wisconsin-project-interview-uzi-rubin-irans-missile-program; Elleman, *Iran's Ballistic Missile Capabilities*, p. 129.

[40] David Albright, *Peddling Peril: How the Secret Nuclear Trade Arms America's Enemies* (New York: Free Press, 2013), pp. 149–51.

[41] Colin H. Kahl, Raj Pattani, and Jacob Stokes, *If All Else Fails: The Challenges of Containing a Nuclear Iran* (Washington DC: Center for a New American Security, 2013), 20–21, 50, 52, https://s3.amazonaws.com/files.cnas.org/documents/CNAS_IfAllElseFails.pdf.

[42] Erik A. Olson, "Iran's Path-Dependent Military Doctrine," *Strategic Studies Quarterly* (Summer 2016), p. 79, http:// www.au.af.mil/au/ssq/digital/pdf/Summer16/Olson.pdf.

[43] Iran, moreover, has shown no interest in confidence- and security-building measures that could reduce the potential for misunderstandings or miscalculation. This is because it believes uncertainty enhances its leverage, while stability would help consolidate an unfavorable status quo. See, for instance, Jay Solomon and Julian E. Barnes, "U.S. Weighs a Direct Line to Iran," *Wall Street Journal*, September 19, 2011, https://www.wsj.com/articles/SB10001424053111903374004576578990787792046; Adm. Mike Mullen, address to the Carnegie Endowment for International Peace, September 21, 2011, http://carnegieendowment.org/files/92011_transcript_Mullen.pdf; Fars News Agency, "Iran Rejects U.S. Hotline Request," November 11, 2012, http://english2.farsnews.com/newstext.php?nn=9107118530.

[44] Uzi Rubin, "Missile Defense and Israel's Deterrence against a Nuclear Iran," in *Israel and a Nuclear Iran: Implications for Arms Control, Deterrence, and Defense*, ed. Ephraim Kam, INSS Memorandum 94

(Tel Aviv: Institute for National Security Studies, 2008),
http://www.inss.org.il/uploadimages/Import/(FILE)1216203568.pdf.

[45] For the implications for Iran of a nuclear exchange, see Cham E. Dallas et al., "Nuclear War between Israel and Iran: Lethality beyond the Pale," *Conflict and Health* 7, no. 10 (May 2013), https://conflictandhealth.biomedcentral.com/articles/10.1186/1752-1505-7-10. See also Michael Eisenstadt, "Glass Houses: Iran's Nuclear Vulnerabilities," Washington Institute for Near East Policy, July 1, 2014, https://www.washingtoninstitute.org/uploads/Documents/pubs/Glass_Houses_final.pdf.

[46] For more on penetration aids and countermeasures, see Uzi Rubin and Azriel Lorber, "Future Trends of Missile Proliferation in the Middle East and Its Impact on Regional Missile Defences," paper presented at the Eighth American Institute of Aeronautics and Astronautics (AIAA) Multinational Conference on Theater Missile Defense, London, June 6–9, 1995.

[47] Bernard Lewis, "August 22: Does Iran Have Something in Store?" *Wall Street Journal*, August 8, 2006, http://www.wsj.com/articles/SB115500154638829470.

[48] See, for instance, Fareed Zakaria, "Deterring Iran Is the Best Option," *Washington Post*, March 14, 2012, https://www.washingtonpost.com/opinions/deterring-iran-is-the-best-option/2012/03/14/gIQA0Y9mCS_story.html; Zbigniew Brzezinski interview on Al Jazeera, "U.S. and Iran: Best of Enemies," Empire, March 31, 2010, http://english.aljazeera.net/programmes/empire/2010/03/201033113196514403.html. For the limitations of Cold War models of deterrence as applied to Iran, see Patrick Clawson and Michael Eisenstadt, eds., *Deterring the Ayatollahs: Complications in Applying Cold War Strategy to Iran*, Policy Focus 72 (Washington DC: Washington Institute, 2007), http://www.washingtoninstitute.org/policy-analysis/view/deterring-the-ayatollahs-complications-in-applying-cold-war-strategy-to-ira.

[49] Clawson and Eisenstadt, eds., *Deterring the Ayatollahs*, http://www.washingtoninstitute.org/policy-analysis/view/deterring-the-ayatollahs-complications-in-applying-cold-war-strategy-to-ira.

[50] Eisenstadt, *The Strategic Culture of the Islamic Republic of Iran*, http://www.washingtoninstitute.org/uploads/Documents/pubs/MESM_7_Eisenstadt.pdf.

[51] Ibid.

[52] Frank Jordans, "Germany Wary of Iran's Nuclear, Missile Procurement Efforts," Associated Press, July 8, 2016, http://bigstory.ap.org/article/1c45e42b0a8340d8b5c62df327aaa817/germany-wary-irans-nuclear-missile-procurement-efforts.

[53] Reuters, "Iranian Revolutionary Guards Fired Rockets near U.S. Warships in Gulf: U.S.," December 29, 2015, http:// www.reuters.com/article/us-usa-iran-warship-idUSKBN0UD00H20151230.

[54] Greg Thielmann, *Iranian Missiles and the Comprehensive Nuclear Deal*, Arms Control Association Iran Nuclear Brief, May 7, 2014, https://www.armscontrol.org/files/Iran_Brief_Iranian_Missiles_Comprehensive_Nuclear_Deal.pdf; Behnam Ben Taleblu, *Iranian Ballistic Missile Tests Since the Nuclear Deal*, Foundation for Defense of Democracies, February 9, 2017, http://www.defenddemocracy.org/content/uploads/documents/20917_Behnam_Ballistic_Missile.pdf; and Iranian and foreign media reports.

[55] Reuters, "U.S. Navy Says It Seized Weapons from Iran Likely Bound for Houthis in Yemen," April 4, 2016, http://www.reuters.com/article/us-iran-usa-yemen-arms-idUSKCN0X12DB.

[56] See, for instance, Bradley Klapper, "U.S. Open to 'New Arrangement' on Iran's Missile Tests," Associated Press, April 7, 2016, http://bigstory.ap.org/article/ff0aa48a68494bdd9cef9b26baba49bf/bahrain-kerry-treads-carefully-human-rights.

[57] Michael Singh, "Iran's Plan to Expand Its Nuclear Program—and Steps the U.S. Can Take to Deter It," *Wall Street Journal*, August 4, 2016, http://www.washingtoninstitute.org/policy-analysis/view/irans-plan-to-expand-its-nuclear-program-and-steps-the-u.s.-can-take-to-det.

[58] Assuming each Iranian missile costs $1–2 million, its full missile inventory is probably worth $1–2 billion. Adding to this the cost of its missile R&D complex, transporter-erector launchers and support vehicles, underground missile facilities, and related infrastructure, the sunken costs of Iran's missile program must amount to several billion dollars—an immense sum considering that Iran's annual defense budget is perhaps $11–15 billion.

[59] Eddie Boxx, "Countering the Iranian Missile Threat in the Middle East," *PolicyWatch* 1991 (Washington Institute for Near East Policy, October 18, 2012), http://www.washingtoninstitute.org/policy-analysis/view/countering-the-iranian-missile-threat-in-the-middle-east.

[60] CDR Jeremy Vaughan, "Deterring Iranian Provocations at Sea," Washington Institute for Near East Policy, *PolicyWatch* 2685, September 12, 2016, http://www.washingtoninstitute.org/policy-analysis/view/deterring-iranian-provocations-at-sea.

[61] Michael Knights, "Responding to Iran's Arms Smuggling in Yemen," Washington Institute for Near East Policy, *PolicyWatch* 2733, December 2, 2016, http://www.washingtoninstitute.org/policy-analysis/view/responding-to-irans-arms-smuggling-in-yemen.

41

[62] Michael Eisenstadt and Michael Knights, "The Battle for Mosul and Iran's Regional Reach," The Washington Institute for Near East Policy, *PolicyWatch* 2735, December 5, 2016, http://www.washingtoninstitute.org/policy-analysis/view/the-battle-for-mosul-and-irans-regional-reach.
[63] Robert Einhorn, *Nonproliferation Challenges Facing the Trump Administration*, The Brookings Institution, Arms Control and Nonproliferation Series Paper 15, March 2017, https://www.brookings.edu/wp-content/uploads/2017/03/acnpi_201703_nonproliferation_challenges_v2.pdf; George Perkovich, "The Iran Deal's Building Blocks of a Better Nuclear Order," Carnegie Endowment for International Peace, June 9, 2016, http://carnegieendowment.org/2016/06/09/iran-deal-s-building-blocks-of-better-nuclear-order-pub-63780; Pierre Goldschmidt, "Looking Beyond Iran and North Korea for Safeguarding the Foundations of Nuclear Proliferation," in Henry Sokolski, ed., *Moving Beyond Pretense: Nuclear Power and Nonproliferation* (Carlisle, PA: Army War College Press, 2014), pp. 311–22.
[64] Michael Eisenstadt, "Glass Houses: Iran's Nuclear Vulnerabilities," https://www.washingtoninstitute.org/uploads/Documents/pubs/Glass_Houses_final.pdf; Michael Eisenstadt, "Speaking about the Unthinkable: The Nuclear Debate Iran Needs to Have," Washington Institute for Near East Policy, *PolicyWatch* 2279, July 1, 2014, http://www.washingtoninstitute.org/policy-analysis/view/speaking-about-the-unthinkable-the-nuclear-debate-iran-needs-to-have.
[65] Michael Eisenstadt, *Deterring an Iranian Nuclear Breakout*, Washington Institute for Near East Policy, Research Note 26, May 2015, http://www.washingtoninstitute.org/uploads/ResearchNote26_Eisenstadt-2.pdf .
[66] Col. Russell J. Hart, Jr., "Defeating Hard and Deeply Buried Targets in 2035," unpublished Air War College paper, Air University, February 15, 2012, http://www.au.af.mil/au/awc/awcgate/cst/bh_2012_hart.pdf.

Ms. ROS-LEHTINEN. Thank you, sir.
Ms. Rosenberg.

STATEMENT OF MS. ELIZABETH ROSENBERG, SENIOR FELLOW AND DIRECTOR, ENERGY, ECONOMICS AND SECURITY PROGRAM, CENTER FOR A NEW AMERICAN SECURITY

Ms. ROSENBERG. Thank you, Chair Ros-Lehtinen, Ranking Member Deutch, distinguished members of the committee. I appreciate the opportunity to testify today on the topic of Iran ballistic missile and IRGC sanctions.

International sanctions on Iran's ballistic missile activities and the IRGC are an integral component to the broad-ranging and powerful financial measures that target and isolate Iran for its nefarious activities. They are at the heart of U.S. sanctions on Iran and set an appropriately aggressive tone for Washington to pursue its interests with this destabilizing regime.

Congress has provided critical leadership in this effort to target Iran's missile activity and the IRGC, and I applaud this important work. I encourage you to continue this attention to make it clear to Iran that while the international community has entered into a strong agreement with Iran over its nuclear program, U.S. policy leaders will aggressively hold Iran accountable for its threatening nonnuclear activities.

The United States has imposed sanctions on the IRGC and Iran's ballistic missile activities specifically to highlight Iran's weapons proliferation, human rights abuses, including through cyber-enabled means, and in the case of the IRGC Quds Force, its support for terrorism.

Even after the nuclear deal, of course, many sanctions on Iran's ballistic missiles development and the IRGC remain firmly in place. U.S. sanctions on Iran's ballistic missile activity seek to expose and counter the agencies and the entities that develop and deploy Iran's missile program. Along with regional missile defense capabilities and the U.S. military's significant presence in the Middle East, as has been mentioned, they are an integral part of the United States effort to deter Iran from using missiles to threaten its neighbors and to protect U.S. interests in the region.

The Iranian missile arsenal is the largest and most lethal in the Middle East, and it is fundamental to the Iranian strategy to project power and influence.

Iran continues its dangerous and provocative missile tests, as you mentioned in your statement, in a show of force. However, the greatest threat that this arsenal presents is the potential for missiles to serve as delivery systems for nuclear weapons, of course.

Financial sanctions imposed by the United States on the IRGC more broadly than just on its missile program target this proliferation activity and its human rights abuse, and in the case of the Quds Force, as I mentioned, its support for terrorism. These various sanctions are important, given the political prominence of the IRGC in Iran and in the Middle East, and its extensive role in a host of Iranian commercial sectors.

However, they have a limited financial impact given the relatively limited links between the U.S. and the Iranian economies and the broad avoidance by Iranians of the U.S. dollar as a means to limit their sanctions exposure. Indeed, the IRGC has been able to function during the last several years of most severe international sanctions pressure on Iran before and leading up to implementation day for the nuclear deal.

The United States has a variety of options to expand sanctions pressure on Iran's ballistic missile activities and the destabilizing and threatening role of the IRGC.

First, the administration should aggressively go after implementing existing sanctions authorities, targeting Iran's ballistic missile procurement networks and the agencies responsible for development and deployment of the missile program.

Second, the administration should immediately embark on a concerted and broad-ranging sanctions campaign to expose and target the dangerous and insidious activities of the IRGC within and beyond the borders of Iran, including exposing the financial activity and holdings of the IRGC, its agents, and instrumentalities and regional terrorist proxies wherever feasible.

The strongest and most successful approach to countering Iranian threats is through continued multilateral action. Where European sanctions on Iranian ballistic missiles and the IRGC do not match those of the United States, U.S. policymakers should strongly urge EU counterparts to align their financial measures.

U.S. leaders should also work with U.N. member states to add new arms or missile proliferators to sanctions lists where there is sufficient information.

Congressional leaders are well placed to outline the contours of such a strategy and to urge aggressive administration implementation. And congressional members can also set the right expectations for successful multilateral engagement, including renewed sanctions pressure, and also a fresh look at force posture arrangements and intelligence and covert activities.

Thank you very much for the opportunity to speak with you today, and I look forward to your questions.

[The prepared statement of Ms. Rosenberg follows:]

Center for a
New American
Security

March 29, 2017

Testimony before the House Committee on Foreign Affairs
Subcommittee on Middle East and North Africa

Testing the Limits: Iran's Ballistic Missile Program, Sanctions, and the
Islamic Revolutionary Guard Corps

Elizabeth Rosenberg, Senior Fellow and Director, Energy, Economics, and Security Program
Center for a New American Security

Chair Ros-Lehtinen, Ranking Member Deutch, distinguished members of the committee, thank you
for the opportunity to testify today on the topic of IRGC and Iran ballistic missile sanctions.

International sanctions on Iran's ballistic missile activities and the Islamic Revolutionary Guard
Corps (IRGC) are an integral component to the broad-ranging and powerful financial measures that
target and isolate Iran for its nefarious activities. They are at the heart of the U.S. sanctions on Iran,
and set an impactful and appropriately aggressive tone for Washington to pursue its interests with
this destabilizing regime. Congress has provided critical leadership in the effort to expose and target
Iran's missile activity and the threatening activities of the IRGC. This includes important oversight
of executive branch activities enforcement of existing financial sanctions authorities. I applaud your
leadership and this important work, and urge your continued attention to make it clear to Iran that
while the international community has entered into a strong agreement with Iran over its nuclear
program, policy leaders, including those in Congress, will aggressively seek to hold Iran to account
for its threatening ballistic missile activity, continued support for terrorism, and regional
destabilization.

Current U.S. Sanctions on Iran's Ballistic Missile Activities and the IRGC

The United States has imposed sanctions on the IRGC and Iran's ballistic missile activities, which
are supported and controlled by the IRGC,[1] pursuant to a variety of legal authorities. These various
designations highlight the IRGC's weapons proliferation, human right abuses, including through
cyber-enabled means, and, in the case of the IRGC's Qods Force, its support for terrorism. While
the nuclear agreement with Iran, the Joint Comprehensive Plan of Action (JCPOA), rolled back
many sanctions on Iran related to its nuclear activities, financial restrictions on entities involved in
Iran's ballistic missile development and the IRGC remain firmly in place. As recently as March 21,

---

[1] Greg Bruno, Jayshree Bajoria, and Jonathan Master, "Iran's Revolutionary Guard," Council on Foreign Relations, June
14, 2013. http://www.cfr.org/iran/irans-revolutionary-guards/p14324.

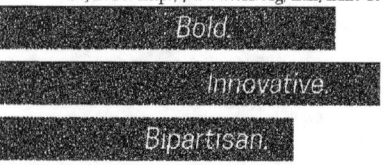

Bold.

Innovative.

Bipartisan.

2017, the Trump administration sanctioned a group of entities and individuals for involvement in the transfer of sensitive items for the country's ballistic missile program.[2] Sanctions such as these prevent U.S. companies and individuals from doing business with Iranian ballistic missile-linked entities or the IRGC. Importantly, remaining secondary sanctions also specifically prevent foreign companies and individuals from doing business in the United States if they do significant business with the IRGC.

Ballistic Missile Sanctions

Sanctions on Iran's ballistic missile activities seek to expose and counter the agencies and entities that develop and deploy Iran's ballistic missile program. Along with regional missile defense capabilities and the U.S. military's significant presence in the Middle East, they are an integral part of the United States' efforts to deter Iran from using missiles to threaten its neighbors and protect U.S. interests in the region. This Iranian missile arsenal is the largest and most lethal in the Middle East, and is fundamental to the Iranian strategy to project power and influence. Perhaps the greatest threat it presents, however, is the potential for these missiles to serve as delivery systems for nuclear weapons. With the JCPOA in place, Iran has agreed to dramatically limit its nuclear enrichment for a number of years. This relegates the most serious concerns about an Iranian nuclear ballistic missile capability to the medium- to longer-term, when provisions in the JCPOA begin to roll off. However, now and in the near term, Iran's missile program presents a threat to U.S. interests and regional stability.

A variety of UN sanctions on Iranian WMD procurement networks and weapons exports remain in place following the JCPOA, but the international body is not aggressively targeting Iran's continuing ballistic missile activities. United Nations Security Council Resolution 2231, the resolution which endorsed the JCPOA and succeeded a series of prior resolutions dealing with Iran's threatening nuclear activities, calls upon Iran "not to undertake any activity related to ballistic missiles designed to be capable of delivering nuclear weapons," for eight years.[3] While an important signifier of international concern over Iran's missile program, it does not require Iran to refrain from ballistic missile activities and is not a ban. Additionally, if Iran claims that it is not working toward nuclear weaponization, then Iran can claim that no ballistic missile activity could be designed to be capable of delivering nuclear weapons. Therefore, some will interpret this to mean that Iran will never be in contravention of this provision of the resolution. Ultimately, this will undermine any serious effort by the Security Council to review or deny any transfer to Iran of goods or technology that could contribute to nuclear weapons delivery systems.

Particularly because the UN's response to Iran's threatening ballistic missile program in Resolution 2231 is relatively limited, many U.S. policymakers seek an aggressive use of national-level sanctions to target Iran's missile proliferation. By imposing U.S. sanctions, leaders in Washington can lead allies in signaling to Iran an international intolerance of Iran's ballistic missile threats. Also, if U.S. policymakers continuously update missile sanctions, regularly adding new designees to U.S.

---

[2] "Iran, North Korea, and Syria Nonproliferation Act Sanctions," U.S. Department of State, media note, March 24, 2017, https://www.state.gov/r/pa/prs/ps/2017/03/269084.htm.
[3] United Nations Security Council (SC), Resolution 2231, July 20, 2015,
http://www.un.org/en/ga/search/view_doc.asp?symbol=S/RES/2231(2015), 99.

sanctions' lists, they can have a meaningful effect on hampering Iranian missile procurement and financing channels. Without this maintenance, it is easy for Iran to form shell companies or front companies to evade sanctions.

IRGC Sanctions

Financial sanctions imposed by the United States on the IRGC are far ranging and include targeting of its ballistic missile proliferation activity,[4] its involvement in human rights abuse,[5] and the support of the IRGC-Qods Force for terrorism and regional destabilization.[6] These various sanctions are important given the political prominence of the IRGC and its extensive role in a host of commercial sectors.[7] However they have a limited financial impact, given the relatively limited links between the U.S. and the Iranian economy, and the broad avoidance by Iranians of the U.S. dollar as a means to limit sanctions exposure. Indeed, the IRGC has been able to function during the last several years despite severe international sanctions placed on Iran resulting in powerful economic pressure.

The IRGC is a powerful organization with control over significant interests in Iran's formal and informal economy. The Treasury Department has called it Iran's "most powerful economic actor."[8] The IRGC may control between 25-60 percent of the formal economy, including assets held directly and those in which it has a stake.[9] The group holds approximately 20 percent of Tehran's Stock Exchange with significant estimated holdings in hundreds of non-publicly traded entities.[10] Its

---

[4] Executive Order 13382 of June 28, 2005, Blocking Property of Weapons of Mass Destruction Proliferators and Their Supporters, Code of Federal Regulations Title 3 (2005): 38567-38579, https://www.state.gov/documents/organization/135435.pdf.

[5] Executive Order 13553 of September 28, 2010, Blocking Property of Certain Persons with Respect to Serious Human Rights Abuses by the Government of Iran and Taking Certain Other Actions, Code of Federal Regulations Title 3 (2010): 60567-60571, https://www.treasury.gov/resource-center/sanctions/Documents/13553.pdf; Executive Order 13606 of April 22, 2012, Blocking the Property and Suspending Entry into the United States of Certain Persons With Respect to Grave Human Rights Abuses by the Governments of Iran and Syria Via Information Technology, Code of Federal Regulations Title 3 (2012): 24571-24574, https://www.treasury.gov/resource-center/sanctions/Programs/Documents/13606.pdf.

[6] Executive Order 13224 of September 23, 2001, Blocking Property and Prohibiting Transactions with Persons Who Commit, Threaten To Commit, or Support Terrorism, Code of Federal Regulations Title 3 (2001): 49079-49083, https://www.treasury.gov/resource-center/sanctions/Documents/13224.pdf.

[7] Alireza Nader, "The Revolutionary Guards," The Iran Primer, United States Institute of Peace, updated August 2015, accessed March 27, 2017, http://iranprimer.usip.org/resource/revolutionary-guards.

[8] "Treasury Submits Report to Congress On NIOC And NITC," U.S. Department of the Treasury, press release, September 24, 2012, https://www.treasury.gov/press-center/press-releases/Pages/tg1718.aspx.

[9] Mark Gregory, "Expanding business empire of Iran's Revolutionary Guards," BBC News, July 28, 2010, http://www.bbc.com/news/world-middle-east-10743580; Abbas Milani, "Taking Tehran's Temperature: One Year On," transcript, (Carnegie Endowment for International Peace, June 8, 2010), http://carnegieendowment.org/files/0609carnegie-tehran.pdf, 5.

[10] Emanuele Ottolenghi, Foundation for Defense of Democracies Center on Sanctions and Illicit Finance, "The Iran Nuclear Deal and its Impact on Iran's Islamic Revolutionary Guards Corps," Hearing before the House Committee on Foreign Affairs Middle East and North Africa Subcommittee, September 17, 2015, http://docs.house.gov/meetings/FA/FA13/20150917/103958/HHRG-114-FA13-Wstate-OttolenghiE-20150917.pdf, 6.

annual income is estimated to be as high as $12 billion per year, about one sixth of the country's GDP.[11]

The IRGC's economic influence is likely even greater than its market capitalization. This is due to the deference that non-IRGC business leaders must pay to the organization,[12] its influential status in the rural economy thanks to its numerous public-works projects,[13] and the IRGC's role in an informal or underground economy, estimated to account for between 6-36 percent of the country's GDP.[14] Furthermore, the IRGC's close ties to the Iranian Supreme Leader and the economically powerful foundations he controls create a dynamic of patronage within and around the IRGC, which vastly enhances the influence of the group.

It is difficult to discern the beneficial owners of many Iranian businesses and commercial entities due to relatively limited, or unenforced, Iranian requirements for disclosure in this jurisdiction. This situation creates an enabling environment for money laundering, tax evasion, corruption, and terrorist financing, which are indeed features of the Iranian economy.[15] For these reasons, Iran has been repeatedly recognized by the Financial Action Task Force,[16] Transparency International,[17] and the World Bank,[18] among others, for egregious financial sector risks and for the difficulty of doing business in this jurisdiction.

In addition to navigating commercial risks, foreign businesses must contend with the difficulty of discerning whether their Iranian business partners are owned or controlled by the IRGC. Only some such entities appear on U.S. or European sanctions lists. However, given the broad reach of the IRGC in the Iranian economy it is likely that many more companies and commercial entities are linked to the IRGC. It is expensive for foreign companies to conduct rigorous due diligence to ascertain whether they are not doing business with the IRGC. Therefore, the expensive legal and reputational risk of violating sanctions often keeps otherwise interested foreign business away.

---

[11] Parisa Hafezi and Louis Charbonneau, "Iranian Nuclear Deal Set To Make Hardline Revolutionary Guards Richer," *Reuters*, July 6, 2015, http://www.reuters.com/article/us-iran-nuclear-economy-insight-idUSKCN0PG1XV20150706.
[12] Robert D. Hormats, "Post-Sanctions Economic Opportunities and Risks in Iran," Issue Brief, (Atlantic Council, February 2016), http://www.atlanticcouncil.org/images/publications/Post-Sanctions_Economic_Opportunities_and_Risks_in_Iran_web_0209.pdf, 8.
[13] Frederic Wehrey, Jerrold D. Green, et al, "The Rise of the Pasdaran: Assessing the Domestic Roles of Iran's Islamic Revolutionary Guards Corps," (The RAND Corporation, 2009), (http://www.rand.org/content/dam/rand/pubs/monographs/2008/RAND_MG821.pdf), 64-66.
[14] Frederic Wehrey, Jerrold D. Green, et al, "The Rise of the Pasdaran: Assessing the Domestic Roles of Iran's Islamic Revolutionary Guards Corps," 55; Emanuele Ottolenghi, Saeed Ghasseminejad, "Who Really Controls Iran's Economy?," *The National Interest*, May 20, 2015, http://nationalinterest.org/feature/who-really-controls-irans-economy-12925?page=2.
[15] Barbara Slavin, "Central Bank Governor: Iran Expects Access to U.S. Financial System," Al-Monitor, April 15, 2016, http://www.al-monitor.com/pulse/originals/2016/04/iran-expects-limited-access-us-financial-system.html.
[16] "FATF Public Statement – 24 February 2017," FATF High-Risk and Non-Cooperative Jurisdictions, February 24, 2017, http://www.fatf-gafi.org/publications/high-riskandnon-cooperativejurisdictions/documents/public-statement-february-2017.html.
[17] "Corruption by Country/Territory: Iran," Transparency International, accessed March 24, 2017, https://www.transparency.org/country/IRN.
[18] "Iran, Islamic Rep," Doing Business (World Bank) Accessed March 24, 2017, http://www.doingbusiness.org/data/exploreeconomies/iran.

The Effects of Sanctions

Ultimately, sanctions on Iran's ballistic missile activities and on the IRGC may be judged to be most successful for their signaling value rather than as a set of measures to strong arm Iranian regime behavior. In periods of sanctions-induced Iranian economic hardship, leaders in Tehran have ensured that its ballistic missile program and the IRGC remain sufficiently well financed to project power and constitute a true threat to regional stability. Domestic Iranian leaders also see value in building this arsenal as a source of national pride. The robust existence and perseverance of these institutions is arguably tied to regime stability.

In the wake of the nuclear deal Iran has expanded its ballistic missile tests in a show of strength and projection of influence.[19] This suggests an Iranian defiance of sanctions and likely constitutes a test of whether U.S. leaders will escalate counter-pressure through expanded sanctions and other means. If the United States does increase sanctions pressure, responding to Iran's recently escalating missile tests, it may have a practical impact in hindering missile procurement activities or some IRGC operations. However, Iran is unlikely to make concessions to reduce the lethality and power of its missile program or the IRGC. Nevertheless, sanctions do have an important place in a strategy to expose and confront Iranian activities of concern and the advancement of U.S. interests in the Middle East.

Options for Expanding Sanctions Pressure on Iran

The United States has a variety of options to expand pressure on Iran pursuant to concerns about Iran's ballistic missile activities and the destabilizing and threatening role of the IRGC. First, the administration should aggressively implement its existing sanctions authorities to go after ballistic missile procurement networks and the agencies responsible for development and deployment of the missile program. Second, the administration should immediately embark on a concerted and broad-ranging sanctions campaign to expose and target the dangerous and insidious activities of the IRGC within and beyond the borders of Iran, including exposing the financial activity and holdings of the IRGC, its agents and instrumentalities, and regional terrorist proxies, wherever feasible.

One strategy that is reportedly under consideration by the administration, and is the subject of currently proposed congressional legislation, is an expansion of sanctions on the IRGC under terrorism authorities. The administration already has broad authorities to target the IRGC with sanctions and punishing financial measures. So, while new terrorism designations specific to Iran would not create any new practical legal or financial effect, it would send a powerful message to Iran and the international community. Foreign allies are not likely to join in such an effort with independent national-level sanctions. However even unilateral U.S. sanctions, and if paired with a strategy to identify and expose IRGC front companies and affiliates, designating the IRGC under terrorism authorities would represent a meaningful new level of rigor to sanctions implementation on Iran.

---

[19] "Iran's Khamenei: Missiles Are Part of the Future," *BBC News,* March 30, 2016, http://www.bbc.com/news/world-middle-east-35925324.

Such new sanctions on the IRGC, or new ballistic missile sanctions, need not--and should not--violate the JCPOA. Deal supporters in Iran and internationally may see a tougher U.S. approach to Iranian ballistic missile activity and support for terrorism as undermining the spirit of the deal. However, this should not be a deterrent for U.S. policy leaders to take strong but calculated action to address Iranian threats and activities. Also, U.S. diplomats should reach out to allies to encourage them to join, rather than reject, a more aggressive approach to targeting Iran's support for terrorism and threatening missile activities. It will be important to underscore to close allies, particularly those also party to the JCPOA, that pushing back on Iran's regional destabilization and support for terrorism can be consistent with tough but continued implementation of the nuclear deal.

The strongest and most successful approach to countering Iranian threats is through continued multilateral action, involving close sanctions coordination between the United States and allies in Europe and Asia. U.S. policy leaders in Congress and in the administration must not lose sight of how important European allies are to successfully countering Iran; actions that weaken the U.S. relationship with Europe will undermine the effort to pressure Iran. Where European sanctions on the Iranian missile program and activities of the IRGC, or its regional proxies including Hezbollah, do not match those of the United States, U.S. policymakers should urge EU counterparts to align their financial measures. The United States should also work with other UN member states to add new arms or missile proliferators to sanctions lists where there is sufficient information and enforce UN travel bans on Qods Force-affiliated individuals. Additionally, U.S. policy leaders should also work with allies in Europe and the Gulf to ensure that the response to Iranian missile provocations is holistic, including a fresh look at sanctions options, force posture arrangements, intelligence and covert activities.

There are some risks associated with adopting new sanctions on Iran's missile program or the IRGC that policymakers should factor into any decision to expand financial pressure. Some analysts have expressed the fear that Iran could retaliate against new missile or IRGC sanctions, attacking or sabotaging U.S. forces in Iraq, with which they share the goal of combatting the Islamic State of Iraq and Syria, or in the Persian Gulf.[20] Some suggest that Iran would use such designations as an excuse to walk away from the JCPOA, laying the blame for its failure at the feet of the United States sanctions crafters. This scenario would likely split U.S. and European allies and make further coordinated action on Iran's nuclear threat, or perhaps on other Iranian activities of concern, extremely difficult. Additionally, others believe that labeling the IRGC a terrorist organization with new sanctions would provoke an even more hostile and escalatory Iranian response and enflame regional tensions.[21]

These are possibilities. However, Iran still has a lot to gain from pursuing the nuclear agreement, including in the realm of slow-moving economic recovery. Iranian leaders also do not seek an aggressive confrontation of military forces with U.S. troops in the Middle East. These reasons diminish the likelihood of an overtly hostile Iranian retaliation for new non-nuclear sanctions. What does seem likely, however, is a hostile political response in Iran that will strengthen hard liners,

[20] Anthony J. Blinken, "Why the Iran Nuclear Deal Must Stand," The New York Times, February 17, 2017, https://www.nytimes.com/2017/02/17/opinion/why-the-iran-nuclear-deal-must-stand.html?_r=1.
[21] Seyed Hossein Mousavian, "Designating Iran's Revolutionary Guards as Terrorists Will Have Dire Consequences," The World Post, February 16, 2017, http://www.huffingtonpost.com/entry/dire-consequences-of-a-terrorist-designation-for-irans_us_58a62065e4b0fa149f9ac39f.

whether or not that serves to unseat pro-JCPOA Iranian President Rouhani in the upcoming national election.

Conclusion

The new administration and Congress have an opportunity to work together to develop and articulate a renewed focus and strategy to address Iran's non-nuclear activities of concern, while preserving the nuclear arms control gains of the JCPOA. The core of this strategy should be a strong U.S. and international response to Iran's escalating ballistic missile tests and the destabilizing role that the IRGC and its terrorist proxies play in the region. Congressional leaders are well placed to outline a U.S. strategy for the sanctions component of such a renewed policy focus, and to urge the administration to aggressively implement authorities in this domain. This strategy should also embrace the principle of multilateralism, with European allies in particular, and involve close coordination between the U.S. Congress and the administration to maximize the credibility, clarity, and effectiveness of Iran policy and regional engagement.

Ms. ROS-LEHTINEN. Thank you to the three of you. Excellent testimony.

Dr. Katzman, I will begin with you. You stated in your written testimony that some are interpreting the JCPOA as essentially walling off core economic sectors in Iran, like energy, banking, manufacturing, from new sanctions. I believe that Iran's core economic sectors are absolutely eligible for impact by nonnuclear-related sanctions under the JCPOA because the IRGC is in control of Iran's ballistic missile programs, as well as so much of Iran's economy. Any effective sanctions targeting the missile program will by necessity impact these core economic sectors.

So do you believe that these economic sectors are walled off from nonnuclear sanctions?

Mr. KATZMAN. Thank you, Congresswoman.

The sanctions that were lifted basically were secondary U.S. sanctions that force major foreign corporations to choose between doing business in Iran with its major economic sectors or doing business in the United States. Those sanctions were lifted in concert with the JCPOA, and we have seen foreign corporations now return.

Some of the big energy majors have returned and are talking about drilling for oil again. Iran's ships are patrolling the seas again, delivering oil. Iran's oil exports are back to where we were in 2011. Iran is back into the international banking system. It has been relinked to the SWIFT electronic payment system. So the Iranian economy has grown, possibly as high as 6 percent in the 1 year since the sanctions were lifted.

So if those sanctions cannot be reimposed like that, it may be difficult to cause Iran to make the calculations on missiles or human rights or terrorism like was made when they accepted the JCPOA. Their economy was hurting so badly that they felt they had to accept the JCPOA. If you cannot reimpose those sanctions at that extensive level, they might not think twice about some of these other activities, yeah.

Ms. ROS-LEHTINEN. Thank you, sir.

And, Mr. Eisenstadt, can you please outline for us the IRGC's involvement in Iran's economy? Which sectors does it have a stake in? And how are they connected to Iran's ballistic missile program? And how can our sanctions against the IRGC and Iran's missile program be more effective?

Mr. EISENSTADT. Madam Chairperson, this is not an area that I am really a specialist in, so I will defer for the most part, except to say my understanding is that the IRGC has involvement throughout just about every sector of the economy. They either have full ownership or partial ownership of firms throughout the economy. Many of them are in sectors that are important, that have a potential contribution to make to the missile program, whether it be related to heavy industry, mining, production of materials that are important potentially for the missile program.

But showing the connection between those industries and the missile program, I think at least in the public domain, is the missing link. And I think therefore any new sanctions regarding the missile program that mandates reporting that exposes these connections would be very helpful.

So let me just say, my approach to sanctions on the missiles, Iran's missile program, is to look at how we can disrupt their ability to acquire special materials, technology, and the like from overseas. And we see in pictures that they continue to publish of missile production facilities that they are getting production technology that they should not be getting under the MTCR, Missile Technology Control Regime. So clearly some of our allies have more work to do in terms of tightening their export controls. So there is more work to be done in that area.

Ms. ROS-LEHTINEN. Thank you.

I don't know if Ms. Rosenberg or Dr. Katzman wanted——

Ms. ROSENBERG. I would be happy to speak to this question, as well as to the question you posed to Mr. Katzman.

Ms. ROS-LEHTINEN. Yes, please.

Ms. ROSENBERG. I would like to affirm your interpretation of the JCPOA, which I also agree does not preclude the United States from pursuing sanctions pursuant to nonnuclear areas of its concern with regard to Iranian behavior. So should there be an entity that is engaged in significant acts of support for terrorism or regional destabilization, the United States can and should pursue sanctions against such an entity. That is different from going after sectors of the Iranian economy which were broadly delisted in the nuclear agreement.

Speaking to the areas of the economy in which the IRGC is involved, they are reported to be quite extensive: Heavy industry, engineering, construction, energy, and shipping. However, as was mentioned, it is difficult to trace the beneficial ownership link between the IRGC and many of its entities in the Iranian economy for various reasons, but such legal requirements for disclosure of this corporate information are not very good in Iran. In fact, that has been pointed out by professional institutions in the financial services sector.

One of the most effective ways that the United States can go after the IRGC for its concerns relating to the IRGC have to do with identifying further agents, entities, companies, fronts, commanders, and business executives in these companies in the economy that work on behalf of the IRGC.

Ms. ROS-LEHTINEN. Thank you, Ms. Rosenberg.

Dr. Katzman, you wanted to comment on that?

Mr. KATZMAN. I would just comment, one of the biggest construction companies in Iran is called Khatam al-Anbiya, which means seal of the prophet. It is called GHORB. It is a designated sanctioned entity. It is very large, thousands of employees. It was started by the IRGC. In fact, it grew out of the IRGC's—like their Army Corps of Engineers. It was the IRGC's construction wing during the Iran-Iraq war, and then it was spun off as essentially a construction company. It is very large and it is a designated entity and it is sanctioned, yes.

Ms. ROS-LEHTINEN. Thank you very much.

Mr. Deutch.

Mr. DEUTCH. Thanks, Madam Chairman.

Dr. Katzman, do you want to just continue with that? So it is already sanctioned and so what more can be done with a huge entity like that.

Mr. KATZMAN. Well, I mean, I think the point is, when the JCPOA was implemented last January, 2016, hundreds of entities were delisted from U.S. sanctions. In other words, they were no longer subject to U.S. sanctions. But these were mainly, again, as I mentioned, energy companies, shipping, shipping insurance, banks, the Central Bank, Iran Air—Iran's civilian economy, delisted.

The IRGC-related companies, like GHORB, other IRGC affiliates, missile entities, anything to do with terrorism, IRGC commanders, I mean, hundreds of entities remain designated for sanctions, and it is in these areas, proliferation, terrorism, human rights. But the civilian economy, Iran's civilian economy, the energy sector, banking, what I mentioned, transportation, sanctions were lifted.

And under the JCPOA, Iran has said that if the sanctions that were lifted are reimposed, Iran would consider that a breach and it would cease implementing its commitment. So, for example, if Iran's Central Bank were again sanctioned to the extent that it was cut off from the international banking system, I think I have a lot of confidence in saying Iran would say the deal is finished. Mr.

DEUTCH. Even if the sanctions had nothing to do with proliferation activity?

Mr. KATZMAN. Correct. The language in the JCPOA is sanctions that were lifted cannot be reimposed for other justifications, non-nuclear. In other words, terrorism, human rights, these other things, cannot be reimposed under other justifications, right.

Mr. DEUTCH. I wanted to just follow up on the concept of multilateral sanctions, which are still I think the best approach, and the frustration of the Security Council to act against the ballistic missile tests. This has now gone on in two administrations. And we raised the tests at the Council and Russia and China played lawyer for Iran and argued that the tests aren't prohibited under 2231.

So if U.N. sanctions aren't an option, what about the EU? And what is the best argument for our EU allies that adopting strong sanctions, ballistic missile sanctions, aren't just of paramount importance to international security, but that they also don't violate the deal—at a time, we should point out, when the EU is interested in vigorously enforcing the deal at least to ensure that the deal remains in place?

Ms. Rosenberg.

Ms. ROSENBERG. Thank you for the question.

I think there is a lot of running room for the United States to work with the EU on sanctions and on further sanctions concerning the IRGC, for example. The EU targets the IRGC under its own sanctions and some of those remain in place still.

It is difficult for the U.N. Security Council, for a number of reasons mentioned already this afternoon, to go after these Iranian missile tests and call them a violation. It doesn't meet the test of the language in the U.N. Security Council resolution and furthermore to the extent that Iran has——

Mr. DEUTCH. They argue that it doesn't meet the test, that is the role they play.

Ms. ROSENBERG. Correct. So if it is difficult to find a violation at that level, then surely the United States and Europe can move forward further here.

I think for the United States offering leadership by designating additional fronts in the network, the procurement network related to the ballistic missile program and working with the EU to share information and asking them to match the sanctions in the EU, by the EU Commission, is a perfectly viable, reasonable, and important strategy for the U.S. to take.

Mr. DEUTCH. Thank you.

Mr. Eisenstadt.

Mr. EISENSTADT. If I could just add, the Islamic Republic has itself said that the U.N. Security Council resolution is something separate than the nuclear deal and they don't consider it binding.

We should say, well, if we are trying to argue for our allies to join us on sanctions related to the missiles, we should say that, look, the Islamic Republic itself says that this is not part of the deal and, therefore, there should not be consideration with regard to our allies. And also we share concern with regard to freedom of navigation in the Gulf and the security of the Gulf and this impinges on that. So I think we have a good argument to make with regard to our European partners.

Mr. DEUTCH. And, Madam Chairman, if I could ask just one other question, and that is in order to weaken the IRGC's involvement in terrorism we have to cut off their access to Hezbollah. And the concern that I know we all share is that as long as Russia continues to turn a blind eye to what Iran is doing in Syria, it makes that really difficult.

Rouhani was just in Moscow this week. Russia, it seems, has accomplished its goal in Syria, being firmly entrenched now in the Middle East. It continues to aid Iran, not just in Syria, but in the uranium sale, the S-300 sale, for reasons that appear to be only to serve their own self-interest or being bulwarks against the United States.

The question I would just put out to you is, if the United States, as the President has now told us repeatedly, wants closer cooperation with Russia, how do we get tough with Iran at the same time? I didn't mean to stump you.

Yes, Ms. Rosenberg.

Ms. ROSENBERG. I don't think that these necessarily must be inconsistent. And whether you appreciate or not the example of the previous administration, there was a demonstration of, on the one hand, working in coordination with Russia and the U.N. process around the nuclear deal, and working aggressively with Russia when it came to application of new sanctions with regard to its activities in Ukraine.

There is no reason why there cannot similarly be a variegated strategy under this administration which could seek to coordinate with Russia as appropriate, perhaps on Syria-related issues, and push back more firmly in this case with regard to support for Iran's ballistic missile program.

Mr. DEUTCH. And Iran's support of Hezbollah and Syria.

Ms. ROSENBERG. Absolutely.

Mr. EISENSTADT. If I could just add to that. I mean, we have worked productively in the past with regard to, say, for instance, the S-300 missiles, delaying the delivery of those for quite some time.

55

The problem is, I think, given the current trajectory of U.S.-Russian relations—and the fact that there is probably some daylight between Russia's position toward the conflict in Syria and Iran's position—but given the general trajectory of U.S.-Russian relations, I think it will be increasingly difficult in the future because of all of the stuff that is going on with regard to hacking and Ukraine and the like, it will be increasingly difficult to find areas to cooperate on. But in principle it is a possibility.

Mr. KATZMAN. If I can just add. In my assessment, it is going to be extremely difficult to get Iran and Hezbollah to be separated. Iran sees Hezbollah as the most prominent outgrowth of the Islamic revolution of 1979. Iran will do anything to defend Hezbollah. I would argue Iran is in Syria in a big way because it wants to protect that weapons channel to Hezbollah. The IRGC created Hezbollah's military wing. The Quds Force grew out of the IRGC's contingent that went to Lebanon to create Hezbollah's military wing.

The connection between Iran and Hezbollah is organic. It would take a tremendous heavy lift to separate these two entities, in my estimation.

Ms. ROS-LEHTINEN. Great questions. Thank you so much, Mr. Deutch.

Mr. Mast of Florida.

Mr. MAST. Mr. Eisenstadt, you spoke in your written testimony about the way Hamas and Hezbollah use their rockets against Israel and that is a useful template for what could happen in the future. And I wanted to start with something backing up a little bit before that.

To what would you attribute this? You know, the United States of America mastered this ballistic technology in the 1950s, 1960s, China did as well, you know, Russia, 1950s, 1960s, 1970s. What would you provide the greatest attribution to, to say this far in the future, 2017, Iran still hasn't mastered that? Why would you say they still haven't mastered that?

Mr. EISENSTADT. One thing that we, I think, often underestimate is exactly how hard it is to even create technologies that we developed in the 1940s and the 1950s for many developing countries today. And so, many proliferators are in some ways along the—if you look at it in terms of proliferation timeline in terms of their capabilities, they are still in the 1940s in many ways.

But you know what, to use a term that my friend Peter Zimmerman coined, while pursuing "bronze medal technology," from their point of view and in terms of their needs it is good enough, because we have seen time and again that even Hamas, with rockets made in home, kind of garage workshops, until the Israelis deployed the Iron Dome, were able to terrorize populations in southern Israel and to harass these people and cause casualties.

So now with the development of Israeli missile defenses, they have developed the ability, at least in—well, in theory and in practice, to intercept these capabilities, but the Iranians are producing them in such numbers and they are cheap relative to the price of defenses, that they have the ability to saturate defenses.

And the Israelis are developing a layered approach, that they have the low end capabilities now with Iron Dome, they have high end with the Arrow, in the middle range they are developing David's Sling and deploying it this year. But most of——

Mr. MAST. To pause you. Are you saying that it was basically pure dumb luck or a lack of intelligence on their part that didn't get them to this point? What about what we have done in modern history, prior to the JCPOA, has prevented them to getting to this point? Prior to that, what prevented them from getting this?

Or even talking about proliferation. You know, the first nuclear weapon, we didn't even have to test Trinity. We knew if you fire one piece of fissile material into another, you are going to get a critical mass. We didn't have to test it.

What has prevented them, previous to the JCPOA, to getting to that point?

Mr. EISENSTADT. It is a combination of efforts to disrupt what they were doing by us, arms control, export control regimes, efforts to try to prevent the spread of this information, although now this stuff is pretty much out there. But it is one thing to know it. It is another thing to actually be able to apply in practice. And you need to have a very large human manpower base, human capital base that is capable of handling complex projects and integrating all the different aspects of it.

We often under-estimate how difficult it. How many countries in the world produce fighter jets or even cars? Iran does produce cars now, but for many years it was kind of knock-down kits that they imported from Peugeot or whatever.

So we often underestimate how difficult it is, these kind of complex industrial tasks. So a lot of it is just that it is extremely hard. We have been doing it for so long—we have what people call tacit knowledge—because we have a lot of people who have learned how to do this kind of thing. But if you are starting from scratch, it is very difficult to be able to master the full range of capabilities needed for a robust ballistic missile program.

Mr. MAST. Where would you say access to the world market puts them in terms of advancing toward what they have yet been able to master? That is China, Russia, U.S., a number of other countries.

Mr. EISENSTADT. Yes, it is very important, because in the 1990s they benefited from Russian help in terms of individuals who were formally associated with Russia's missile programs. Their Shahab-3 missile was based on the North Korean Nodong. So they have gotten help from the North Koreans, the Russians, and also China was involved in their solid fuel rocket program.

So they have benefited from foreign assistance and they probably still do. Every program around the world has benefited from foreign assistance. But they have reached a point now where they have in some ways surpassed their former teachers in North Korea and they are generally considered to be more capable in this area than the North Koreans in most areas in the missile realm.

But getting know-how and materials from abroad is still very important for their program, and there are some areas where I think they will continue to benefit. For instance, penetration aids and countermeasures, which as far as we know they don't really put on their missiles yet. That is the next step and that will make missile defense much harder if they are able to jam and put out counter-measures to the missile defenses.

Mr. MAST. We didn't get into MIRV or anything else, but my time has expired.

Ms. ROS-LEHTINEN. Thank you, Mr. Mast.

I will follow up with some of your questions. Mr.——

Mr. SUOZZI. Suozzi.

Ms. ROS-LEHTINEN. Suozzi.

Mr. SUOZZI. You have got it.

Ms. ROS-LEHTINEN. I have got a really difficult name. So I hope you don't get insulted by Suozzi.

Mr. SUOZZI. Suozzi, in Italian.

Madam Chair, I want to thank you very much for your leadership here, as well as the ranking member.

I want to thank the witnesses for their thoughtful insight and analysis. It really is a great education that you are giving us here today.

I think there is broad agreement in this room that there is a serious problem with Iran's ballistic missile program and that something has to be done. It is a question of, what is the proper authority, and how are we going to do it, and who are our partners going to be in that process? But I think that there is broad agreement. I want to ask a question about timing. The elections are coming up in Iran in May. I would like to just hear the benefit of your analysis regarding the politics of Iran and how the President, Rouhani, and the Supreme Leader and the IRGC and all the different players that are involved here—the regular military—just tell me a little bit about the intersection of all them and then how what we do could or could not affect that outcome.

Mr. KATZMAN. I will start with that. The regular military that existed under the Shah, it is still there. It does not interfere in politics at all. In fact, during the uprising of 2009, the regular military issued a letter saying, "Do not ask us to go repress these demonstrators." So they are not a factor.

Now the IRGC, as I said in my statement, is a factor.

Mr. SUOZZI. Does the regular military report to the civilian President?

Mr. KATZMAN. It reports up to the general headquarters that reports to the Supreme Leader, actually.

Mr. SUOZZI. To the Supreme Leader. Okay.

Mr. KATZMAN. Yes. The Supreme Leader is technically the commander in chief of the whole Armed Forces, right.

The IRGC does interfere in politics, and they have done so on several occasions. In fact, it was widely reported, and there seems to be agreement, that it did put Mr. Ahmadinejad over the top in 2005. He came out of nowhere. But the IRGC deployed the Basij. They leafleted for him. They drove people to the polls. And they view it as their mission to interfere in politics to defend the revolution.

Now, I think most experts—and I would say I am in this camp too—think if it is a free and fair election, Mr. Rouhani is the favorite. He ran on a platform of delivering Iran from its international isolation. He negotiated the JCPOA. He did bring them, to some extent, out of their isolation. So the people that voted for him in 2013 seem to probably vote for him again.

Now, the issue is the hardliners. There was some thinking earlier on that the hardliners would maybe just not even contest it so much. But no. They seem to be organizing. They are trying to unify around one conservative hardline candidate to oppose him.

Mr. SUOZZI. Who is that?

Mr. KATZMAN. Well, they are having some caucuses, for the first time, they are actually having some meetings to try to vote on one unified candidate. The issue is there is one particular figure who the Supreme Leader favors a lot who they might choose. And that would be significant because, if this individual runs, the regime might be tempted to try to, let's say, interfere on his behalf, to put it mildly. He is the leader of the Quds Razavi Foundation in Mashhad. Khamenei appointed him last summer. And Khamenei appears to favor him as the next Supreme Leader. So engineering him to the Presidency would give him an advantage to be the next Supreme Leader.

Mr. EISENSTADT. If I could take a——

Mr. SUOZZI. I am sorry. Does it help or hurt for us to do something before May?

Mr. KATZMAN. You mean in terms of sanctions? Well, probably the hardliners, the Supreme Leader, they have been criticizing Rouhani to some extent that he—they are saying he has not delivered all the promises of sanctions relief. It is possible that new action——

Mr. SUOZZI. I am running out of time.

Mr. Eisenstadt, go ahead.

Mr. EISENSTADT. I will just be quick. Iran's domestic politics has its own internal logic. And our ability to influence it in ways that redounds to the benefit of American policy has generally worked out, you know, just the opposite that we had hoped. And I would just say we could probably do a lot to hurt things. But there is not a lot we can do to help the people that we want to help.

You know, President Khatami, when he was elected in 1997, we had hopes that this would herald a change. He was undercut by his domestic opponents. President Bush wanted regime change, but the people didn't rise up. They rose up in 2009, when we had a President who wanted to engage the regime there.

And with the JCPOA, we were hoping that the nuclear agreement would lead to a broadened—you know, a general improvement in the relations between the two countries. But what we have seen is in fact it has probably emboldened those who are against the improvement of relations. So our ability to game this in a way to achieve—to advance our goals has been shown to be very limited, if nonexistent.

But there are things we can do that could harm things if we act in a heavy-handed way sometimes. But often we can't really help the people we want to help usually.

Ms. ROSENBERG. I will just be very brief in responding to this. I would like to agree with the comments just made by my colleague, Dr. Eisenstadt, that in fact it is very difficult for U.S. policymakers to specifically engineer particular political outcomes in Iran. We should be very humble about that.

I don't think that undertaking sanctions enforcement using existing authorities will meaningfully sway Iranian politics. It doesn't actually change the broader U.S. posture or the set of authorities that are in place. Nevertheless, there is no specific need to do something now versus 60 or 90 days from now, absent a particular provocation against which the U.S. should push back.

There are plenty of opportunities. The United States has an ability to use them whenever it wants.

Mr. SUOZZI. Thank you very much.

Ms. ROS-LEHTINEN. Thank you very much, sir. Excellent questions and answers.

Now we turn to Mrs. Wagner—Ambassador Wagner.

Mrs. WAGNER. Thank you, Madam Chairman.

Mr. Eisenstadt, the rules of Iranian cyber warfare seem to deviate I think from the codes that guide the world's five cyber powers: The U.S., U.K., Russia, China, and Israel. Iranian hackers do not just engage in espionage and gather intelligence; they try to do harm. There were some reports last spring that there had been a lull in Iranian cyber activities since the nuclear deal. Can you discuss, to the best of your ability, how Iranian cyber strategy has shifted in the wake of the nuclear deal and how Iran will use destructive cyber capabilities in the future?

Mr. EISENSTADT. Yeah. A lot of this will be necessarily speculative. My understanding is that, during the negotiation of the JCPOA, they actually held in abeyance a lot of their offensive cyber activities. After its conclusion, my understanding is that there was—they resumed a lot of their net reconnaissance activities. In other words, they were kind of snooping around to try to gather information about critical infrastructure in the United States and elsewhere, both probably to send the signal that they have the capability to harm us in this domain in the future should relations deteriorate and also to build up their cyber target folders.

And a lot of this also involved spear-phishing activities against personnel involved in American Iran policy and the like.

There were also some attacks directed against Saudi Arabia over the winter, which probably are related to the worsening or the downturn in relations between Saudi Arabia and Iran.

So, from Iran's point of view, a lot of their activities are in response to aggressive action either by the United States and Israel, for instance, with regard to Stuxnet, or other activities that were done, for instance the sanctions against their financial sector; so they attacked our financial sector with denials of service activities, and, likewise, they engaged in attacks on Saudi Aramco and Qatar's RasGas in response to our sanctions on their oil industry a few years ago.

So, from their point of view, a lot of it has been defensive thus far, but I have no doubt that if there was a kind of deterioration in relations with Iran—from their point of view, we live in a cyber glass house. We have massive critical infrastructure which, right now, we don't have the ability to protect. Their capabilities are not advanced; they are kind of a third-tier cyber power. But I think they have great potential in this area. But this is an area which, in the future, I think will be much more important for them. Right now, there is not probably—they could do some—they could be a nuisance at this time, and perhaps more.

Mrs. WAGNER. I have great concerns about our future and where we may be going with this.

Moving on, it seems that Erdogan has long been loath to criticize Iranian ballistic missile and nuclear programs. The complicated relationship between Turkey and Iran has become more concerning with the Moscow Declaration and the trial of Turkish-Iranian sanctions-buster Reza Zarrab in New York.

Ms. Rosenberg, given the arrest of Turkish sanctions-busters in the U.S. and the information that courts may uncover, do you think we will find that the Turkish elite have extensive Iranian ties?

Ms. ROSENBERG. Ties to Iran or ties to sanctions evasion?

Mrs. WAGNER. Yes.

Ms. ROSENBERG. That is a subject that has been of great concern and focus for U.S. policy leaders and for the U.S. intelligence community. There has been quite a lot of investigation into this, appropriately so, given economic linkages and also political ties. I should say that Turkey is not singled out in this category. There are other jurisdictions where linkages between high-level officials and economic linkages put——

Mrs. WAGNER. But you would say there are ties there?

Ms. ROSENBERG. There are links, and the concern is they may be more insidious than merely political or commercial ties could suggest.

Mrs. WAGNER. Interesting. Okay.

So, Mr. Eisenstadt, in my short time here—or others on the panel—to what extent does Iranian money fund terror groups operating inside of Turkey?

Mr. EISENSTADT. I will defer to my colleagues. I don't follow Turkey very closely. So I will defer to others on this.

Mr. KATZMAN. You are talking about Kurdish groups?

Mrs. WAGNER. Yes.

Mr. KATZMAN. The IRGC has some relation with the Iraqi Kurds. PKK—not sure—not really a close connection there.

Mrs. WAGNER. Ms. Rosenberg? I know my time is up.

Ms. ROSENBERG. I have nothing further to add.

Mrs. WAGNER. Thank you very much, Madam Chair. I yield back.

Ms. ROS-LEHTINEN. Thank you very much, Mrs. Wagner. You make a valuable contribution to our subcommittee.

Mr. Kinzinger, thank you for your service also on our subcommittee and to our Nation.

Mr. KINZINGER. It is good to be back. Thanks.

Thank you all for being here. Obviously, I think it comes as no surprise I thought the JCPOA was a pretty bad deal. I think it really just provides, as we look at it, a roadmap for a timeline on how to acquire nuclear weapons eventually. And when it comes to playing the long game, I think Iran is okay with saying, "We can have weapons in 10 or 15 years," or the threat of weapons is almost, in many cases, as good as having them.

But I also think now, obviously, we are in a situation where to redevelop, despite the discussion of snapback provisions and sanctions, which we knew would never happen, being able to develop a coalition of people to reengage Iran through that would be difficult. But I think we have to watch this JCPOA like a hawk and be ready to fight back against any violations and push back against ballistic missile technology.

I also think, when you look at Iran—and it is not just what is happening in Yemen—I think what is extremely important is what is happening in Syria. And you look at Bashar al-Assad, who I actually believe created ISIS, not necessarily by signing on the dotted line somewhere, but by creating an environment where it is easy to recruit into Daesh or ISIS from. So I believe that Iran bears some responsibility for the existence of ISIS.

Now, I also want to say—I am co-chair of the Iraq Caucus and, you know, obviously, an Iraq veteran myself. And when I was in Iraq, we saw the role of Iran and Iraq very closely. We know that hundreds of Americans died as a result of Iran's involvement in Iraq. And we know that, in fact, the incoming Iranian Ambassador is a senior IRGC official. So we can only estimate what that means. We cannot allow Iran to continue to destabilize Iraq.

So, in addition to sanctions, Mr. Eisenstadt, how would you advise the administration to counter Tehran's influence in Iraq?

Mr. EISENSTADT. First of all, the first thing I would recommend is that we commit to make it clear to the Iraqis—let me just say that the Iraqi Government, both the current government and even the previous government under Nouri al-Maliki, has always wanted to maintain a balance between the United States and Iran. And indicating to them that we want to maintain a long-term security relationship with them as well as a relationship in other areas will make it clear to them that they will have the ability to continue with that policy.

We have to recognize, because of proximity, they have to make their peace with the Iranians and live with a certain degree of influence that many Iraqis feel uncomfortable with. Making it clear that we want a long-term security relationship with them is the first part of that. I think committing to a long-term training relationship with the Iraqi Armed Forces—I mean, one of the things that has come through with this campaign in Mosul is that it was—basically, while, in the early days after June 2014, the Popular Mobilization Forces were very important for breaking the advance of ISIL, the conventional military forces have been key to pushing them back in most places. And I think we can make a very convincing case to the Iraqi Government that you need to continue building up your conventional security forces, and we are really the ideal partner to do that. Iran can't help you there.

So, basically, there are things we can do, I think, in this regard to continue to ensure that Iraq knows that we want this relationship, and they will be able to push back.

Mr. KINZINGER. That is important to know, too, is the Iraqi military can be fully capable, but they need the American military to stiffen their spine at least for now. And we see, obviously, that was important in the fight against Daesh.

Ms. Rosenberg, I want to ask you about Syria. Again, 500,000 dead Syrians almost, 50,000 of which are children. You are watching Iran use, I think, money from sanctions relief to prop up that regime. And, unfortunately, around the world, there is kind of this belief now that it is either Bashar al-Assad or it is terrorism, and

I don't think people recognize that, in fact, Assad is creating the next generation of terrorists right now—that we will end up having to fight—by taking away opportunity and freedom for people.

But, specifically, when I talk about the sanctions relief and the money, do you know if there is any way we can track how much that money is being used in Iran? And if they are using that to fund genocides, what kind of action can we take to punish them? Ms. ROSENBERG. Thank you for the question. It is difficult, as I think you are indicating, to track exactly where Iran's money that was unfrozen after the nuclear deal is going or is flowing specifi- cally.

That is true for a number of reasons. Two key ones are that, if we are talking about state revenues, it goes into a state budget and can be allocated under the design of the state. So there is not a transaction chain to follow if it were going through independent institutions that must use private banking channels, et cetera.

Another significant reason that it is difficult to understand ex- actly where it is flowing is because Iran has ample reason to keep that money outside of its own jurisdiction and not to repatriate it and then to hand it over, in this instance, to President Assad in terms of cash or material support, using this to defend its currency, using it to balance international trade. Iran still struggles for ac- cess to hard currency. So there is quite ample reason for it to use this for what is essentially the civilian economy. There are great needs there in order to deliver economic relief to the population, which was a mandate, of course, of President Rouhani as part of this deal and following on.

Mr. KINZINGER. Thank you.

With that, I will yield back.

Ms. ROS-LEHTINEN. Thank you so much, Mr. Kinzinger.

And Mr. Schneider of Illinois. Thank you.

Mr. SCHNEIDER. Thank you.

And, again, thank you to the witnesses for your testimony.

Dr. Katzman, in your opening statement, you talked a bit about Iran's calculus and trying to change their calculus. If I think about math briefly, on the right-hand side of the equation are goals and objectives for Iran. Broadly speaking, that is preserving the regime and maintaining their influence. On the left-hand side of that equation are factors they control and factors they don't control— hopefully we can. Now, ultimately, it is up to everybody. What are the factors post or within the context of the JCPOA, within the context of what is happening in Syria, in Yemen, and around the region, with broad context of what is happening in our country and around the world—what can we do to change that calculus? And what do we have to understand about Iran's thinking to know which levers to pull or which buttons to push?

Mr. KATZMAN. I would just start by saying Iran's calculus is multifaceted in the region. As I said in my statement, Iran views the Middle East as controlled basically by the United States, Israel, and Saudi Arabia. That is how they think, which is a power struc- ture, in Iran's view, that is weighted against Shia, against Islamist parties, against anyone that is not part of the dominant elite. So they have chosen to intervene in a number of places to protect na- tional interests, to protect their allies, to protect favored parties. And what is really needed is a multifaceted approach.

Obviously, I think if all the conflicts we see going in Syria, in Yemen, in Iraq were ended, then Iran might not have rationale to be intervening as it is.

Mr. SCHNEIDER. I suspect they would find other rationales.

Mr. Eisenstadt, your thoughts?

Mr. EISENSTADT. I just want to build on Ken's comments before about Iran and Hezbollah. I agree that we probably can't separate Iran from Hezbollah, but we haven't increased costs for Iran for its involvement in Syria. Our train-and-equip program with the Syrian opposition in the past was really not a serious effort. It may be too late now for us to mount a serious effort. But I would argue that we need to find people among the non-Salafist opposition to arm, both in order to ensure that areas where there are ceasefires remain ceasefires—because if the regime is able to build up its strength, it won't keep these ceasefires over time—and in areas where there aren't ceasefires and the regime continues to fight, we increase the costs for them and their allies, which includes the Iranians. And if this becomes a long-term quagmire for Iran, which this may be something which we don't have the ability to do now, but if we were able to do that, we might also be able to drive a wedge between Iran and Russia because I don't think—Russia has, I think, different interests in Syria than the Iranians do.

But we need to have a cost-imposing strategy in Syria, which we have not really tried until now. And I would hope this current administration might consider that going forward.

Mr. SCHNEIDER. I will come to you, Ms. Rosenberg, in a second. But, Mr. Eisenstadt, I need you to talk about Hezbollah. Is it fair to say that HIFPA, the Hezbollah International Financing Prevention Act, has had an impact on Hezbollah's ability to act in the region, or are there more things we can do around that as well?

Mr. EISENSTADT. My understanding is it has had a major impact but perhaps not on their ability to act in the region, because I think, in terms of prioritizing moneys, from their point of view, their activities in Syria and elsewhere is existential, from their point of view, and if they have less money for social services and to provide for their base, well, in terms of guns and butter, the money goes to the guns and not the butter at this point. But in the long term, that could have an impact in terms of how their domestic support base looks at them if they can't benefit from this in the future.

Mr. SCHNEIDER. Ms. Rosenberg.

Ms. ROSENBERG. I would just add briefly to that, in addition to raising the costs, I think that creating greater leverage for the United States and other international allies can be cultivated by exposing—further exposing—Iran's dangerous activities or naked violations of arms restrictions, for example. What I am talking about here is using sanctions as a means to expose particular violations or circumvention activities, doing more public interdiction of weapons for Houthis or to proxies, terrorist proxies, in the Middle East, and again through possibly use U.S. force posture and protection in the Middle East by identifying instances where Iran is engaged in threatening behavior, saber rattling in the Gulf and in the straits.

Mr. SCHNEIDER. Thank you.

With that, my time is all but expired. I will yield back.

Ms. Ros-LEHTINEN. Thank you very much, Mr. Schneider.

Now, Mr. Connolly of Virginia.

Mr. CONNOLLY. Thank you, Madam Chairman, and thank you so much for pulling this together.

Wonderful panel. I wish we had lots of time with each one of you because I have enjoyed listening to the testimony and watching it.

I am going to go kind of rapid fire. Bear with me because I only have got 5 minutes, and this chairman is tight.

Ms. Ros-LEHTINEN. No, no, no. Take all the time you want.

Mr. CONNOLLY. Ms. Rosenberg, you answered Mr. Deutch's question about the apparent incompatibility of the Trump administration's desire for a rapprochement with Russia with Iranian threats. You said these don't need to be inconsistent. And I want to give you a chance to explain that because, to me, there is prima facie evidence they are inherently inconsistent. I mean, their support for Houthis, their support for Hezbollah, their support for Assad: These are all goals antithetical to U.S. policy that has not changed with the new administration—that I am aware of.

And what did you mean they don't need to be inconsistent? How could they be otherwise? I am not trying to challenge you. I want to give you an opportunity to clarify.

Ms. ROSENBERG. Sure. What I meant was that on U.S. posture toward Russia there could be both cooperation in certain domains and a tough pushback in others.

Mr. CONNOLLY. Even where we disagree.

Ms. ROSENBERG. Correct.

Mr. CONNOLLY. Got it. That is what you meant.

Ms. ROSENBERG. Yes.

Mr. CONNOLLY. Thank you.

Dr. Katzman, how important do you believe, in resolving all of these issues ultimately—what is going on in Yemen, the civil war in Syria, and other tensions in the region; I could go down the laundry list—how important, at the end of the day, will diplomacy be as part of the solution?

Mr. KATZMAN. Well, actually——

Mr. CONNOLLY. Could you speak up?

Mr. KATZMAN. It was tried. After the JCPOA, there was in fact an effort to enlist Iran to try to get——

Mr. CONNOLLY. No. I am talking about our diplomacy.

Mr. KATZMAN. Well, the U.S. tried to—we were talking with the Iranians after the JCPOA was finalized to get them to be helpful on Syria. It did not succeed. The JCPOA still went forward, but that did not succeed because Iran's interests were just completely different. They need Assad there because he is allowing this channel for Iran to support Hezbollah, which is their most cherished goal. So the Iranians did not cooperate. We tried diplomacy, and it did not succeed in that particular example.

Mr. CONNOLLY. Fair enough. But although that kind of goes back to Ms. Rosenberg's point—we agree on some things; we are going to disagree on others—it really depends on what is in—perceived national interest. Apparently Iran perceived that a nuclear agreement was in its interests.

Mr. KATZMAN. They absolutely did.

Mr. CONNOLLY. As did we and the other world powers.

Mr. KATZMAN. The sanctions drove them into what we here, if it had done that much damage to our economy, it was on the line of the Great Depression here.

Mr. CONNOLLY. Thank you. Very good point.

And that allows me to segue to Mr. Eisenstadt, and you can comment as well. How efficacious will sanctions be, can they be, on the issue of ballistic missiles and other unacceptable behavior by Iran? It seemed to work on the nuclear front. Can it, will it work here? Mr.

EISENSTADT. I think the case of the nuclear sanctions are kind of sui generis at this point. And I think the best we could hope for is kind of incremental benefits, disrupting their efforts to acquire technology, know-how, and the like, small wins, if you will. The JCPOA gave us, if it works as intended, perhaps 15 years of respite in which we could use the time to perhaps change Iran's nuclear calculus. With the missiles, it is going to be an ongoing kind of thing with small victories at best.

Mr. CONNOLLY. When you said "sui generis," part of that is we actually had, mirabile dictu, the cooperation of Russia and China and France. On ballistic missiles and other behavior, we clearly will not.

Mr. EISENSTADT. Yes. I agree, yes.

Mr. CONNOLLY. Very good point. Either one of you, Ms. Rosenberg or Dr. Katzman, want to comment on that? This is very relevant to us, as the chairman knows, because we are, as we speak, looking at additional sanctions legislation.

Ms. ROSENBERG. Sure. I would add that——

Mr. CONNOLLY. If you can speak into that microphone like Dr. Katzman did.

Ms. ROSENBERG. In addition to sanctions that can and should be part of the strategy, I certainly agree that, as a kind of creation of leverage or means to cultivate U.S.—for deterrence for Iran, these are small by comparison to a conventional deterrence force, which underscores the point that sanctions must be part of a broader, more holistic strategy of alliance, politics, and operational activities, as well as conventional defenses, not to mention cyber activity, covert activity.

And this body, Congress, is well positioned to oversee not just sanctions, of course, but other—these other realms as well, particularly force structure and appropriations.

Mr. CONNOLLY. Madam Chairman, if you would just allow Dr. Katzman to respond, and then I will yield back. I thank the chair.

Mr. KATZMAN. I would say that——

Mr. CONNOLLY. You have got to speak into the microphone again, Dr. Katzman.

Mr. KATZMAN. I sort of lost my train of thought.

Mr. CONNOLLY. Sorry. "I would say," you started to say.

Mr. KATZMAN. What was the question again? I am sorry.

Mr. CONNOLLY. I think were you about to say, "I would say that was a brilliant question, Congressman Connolly, and God, I wish this hearing had been having more like that," something like that. No? That wasn't it. I was trying to help you here.

Mr. KATZMAN. I mean, I would say sanctions were effective in getting the JCPOA because they affected Iran's core economic—its

66

economy, its entire civilian economy. To work at the margins, to have other sanctions that are only going to nibble at the margins of Iran's economy are not likely to affect Iran's calculations.

Mr. CONNOLLY. Would you agree with Mr. Eisenstadt that in some ways the sanctions with respect to the nuclear development program were sui generis?

Mr. KATZMAN. Yes.

Mr. CONNOLLY. And, therefore, unlikely to be replicated for anything else?

Mr. KATZMAN. Well, if the new administration decides that it is going to implement the JCPOA, Iran is very clear that if the sanctions that were lifted are reimposed under other justifications, Iran is going to walk away from the deal. Iran is very clear on that.

Mr. CONNOLLY. Well, let me just say: There are many of us up here who support the JCPOA, who believe fervently the JCPOA is working, that, as a matter of fact, the existential threat to Israel was denial of JCPOA, not approval, and will not support sanctions that encroach on—that we won't do. I am more than willing to look at sanctions in the other venues. But I always worry with respect to sanctions about efficacy. And that is why I take what Mr. Eisenstadt said seriously. It doesn't mean don't do it, but if we are going to do it, it can't just be a feel-good, symbolic kind of thing. It has to be toward some end, a change in behavior. And that was the nature of my question.

Mr. KATZMAN. Let me just give you—Iran was exporting 2.6 million barrels a day of oil. When the sanctions kicked in, Iran was reduced to 1 million barrels a day, 60 percent decrease. That is what caused, that type of diminishment is what caused Iran to make a new calculation. Unless you can replicate that, it is going to be very difficult to get Iran to make a new calculus.

Mr. CONNOLLY. Excellent point. And we even got nations like India to agree—think about this—to reduce Iran as a supplier of something they don't really produce. That is a big hardship. And to get that level of cooperation takes a lot of diplomatic and other skills. And I take Mr. Eisenstadt's point: Not so easy to replicate that for other things. We can try, but that is going to be a bigger challenge.

Mr. Eisenstadt?

Mr. EISENSTADT. Can I make just one more point? Also, depending upon how U.S. relations with Russia and China evolve, even if Iran was to violate its JCPOA commitments, I am not sure we would even be able to snap back sanctions a few years from now. The stars all aligned in the last couple years to enable JCPOA and the sanctions. And politics might evolve in a certain way that it may not be possible in the future even for nuclear violations.

Mr. CONNOLLY. Good point.

Madam Chairman, you have been very indulgent. And I really appreciate it, but I think this is a really important discussion. Thank you for putting this together.

Ms. ROS-LEHTINEN. You are right, especially in terms of new legislation that is building up in Congress.

Thank you, Mr. Connolly, as always.

And thank you to our witnesses.

With that, our subcommittee is adjourned. Thank you.

[Whereupon, at 3:37 p.m., the subcommittee was adjourned.]

APPENDIX

MATERIAL SUBMITTED FOR THE RECORD

SUBCOMMITTEE HEARING NOTICE
COMMITTEE ON FOREIGN AFFAIRS
U.S. HOUSE OF REPRESENTATIVES
WASHINGTON, DC 20515-6128

Subcommittee on the Middle East and North Africa
Ileana Ros-Lehtinen (R-FL), Chairman

March 23, 2017

TO: MEMBERS OF THE COMMITTEE ON FOREIGN AFFAIRS

You are respectfully requested to attend an OPEN hearing of the Committee on Foreign Affairs, to be held by the Subcommittee on the Middle East and North Africa in Room 2172 of the Rayburn House Office Building (and available live on the Committee website at http://www.ForeignAffairs.house.gov):

DATE: Wednesday, March 29, 2017

TIME: 2:00 p.m.

SUBJECT: Testing the Limits: Iran's Ballistic Missile Program, Sanctions, and the Islamic Revolutionary Guard Corps

WITNESSES: Kenneth Katzman, Ph. D.
Specialist in Middle Eastern Affairs
Congressional Research Service

Mr. Michael Eisenstadt
Kahn Fellow
Director of Military and Security Studies Program
The Washington Institute for Near East Policy

Ms. Elizabeth Rosenberg
Senior Fellow
Director of Energy, Economic and Security Program
Center for a New American Security

By Direction of the Chairman

The Committee on Foreign Affairs seeks to make its facilities accessible to persons with disabilities. If you are in need of special accommodations, please call 202/225-5021 at least four business days in advance of the event, whenever practicable. Questions with regard to special accommodations in general (including availability of Committee materials in alternative formats and assistive listening devices) may be directed to the Committee.

COMMITTEE ON FOREIGN AFFAIRS

MINUTES OF SUBCOMMITTEE ON _____*The Middle East and North Africa*_____ HEARING

Day___*Wednesday*___Date___*January 29th, 2017*___Room_____*2172*_____

Starting Time ___*2:06 p.m.*___ Ending Time ___*3:37 p.m.*___

Recesses [_____] (_____to_____) (_____to_____) (_____to_____) (_____to_____) (_____to_____) (_____to_____)

Presiding Member(s)

Chairman Ileana Ros-Lehtinen

Check all of the following that apply:

Open Session ☑   Electronically Recorded (taped) ☐
Executive (closed) Session ☐   Stenographic Record ☑
Televised ☑

TITLE OF HEARING:

Testing the Limits: Iran's Ballistic Missiles, Sanctions, and the Islamic Revolutionary Guard Corps

---

SUBCOMMITTEE MEMBERS PRESENT:

GOP - Reps. Chabot, DeSantis, Kinzinger, Zeldin, Wagner, Mast, Fitzpatrick
DEM- Ranking Member Deutch, Reps. Connolly, Cicilline, Boyle, Gabbard, Schneider, Suozzi, Lieu

---

NON-SUBCOMMITTEE MEMBERS PRESENT: *(Mark with an * if they are not members of full committee.)*

HEARING WITNESSES: Same as meeting notice attached? Yes ☑ No ☐
(If "no", please list below and include title, agency, department, or organization.)

STATEMENTS FOR THE RECORD: *(List any statements submitted for the record.)*

Representative Gerald Connolly's Statement for the Record

TIME SCHEDULED TO RECONVENE _____
or
TIME ADJOURNED ___*3:37 p.m.*___

_____
Subcommittee Staff Associate

Statement for the Record
Submitted by Mr. Connolly of Virginia

Iran's ballistic missile program poses a serious threat to the national security interests of the U.S. and our closest allies. The Islamic Republic possesses the largest and most diverse ballistic missile inventory in the Middle East, and it has built this deadly arsenal with the help of other global bad actors, namely North Korea. Iran has distributed short-range missiles to regional terrorist organizations that in turn use them against Israel. Tehran's long-range missile systems threaten to strike our NATO allies. Iran continues to conduct ballistic missile tests that imperil U.S. ships, forces, and allies in the Persian Gulf.

The greatest and, potentially, existential threat posed by Iran's ballistic missile program is the development and deployment of a nuclear-armed ballistic missile. This is a threat the international community has a shared interest in eliminating. To that end, through a combination of concerted international diplomacy and pressure, the Obama Administration successfully negotiated the Joint Comprehensive Plan of Action (JCPOA), which effectively blocks Iran's path to developing a nuclear weapon. And the good news is that the JCPOA is working. Iran is meeting its obligations under the deal. However, the JCPOA is not, and never claimed to be, an all-encompassing agreement that addresses each and every malign action of the government in Tehran.

We must be clear that the United States takes seriously Iran's destabilizing provocations and lay out a strategic response that holds Iran accountable without violating U.S. obligations under the Iran nuclear agreement. Iran's repeated testing of ballistic missiles runs contrary to the United Nations Security Council Resolution 2231, which calls upon Iran "not to undertake any activity related to ballistic missiles designed to be capable of delivering nuclear weapons, including launches using such ballistic missile technology." Iran's Islamic Revolution Guard Corps (IRGC) continues to bankroll and arm regional terrorist organizations, including Hezbollah and Hamas, that threaten our greatest ally in the Middle East, Israel. Iran further acts as a destabilizing force in the region by supporting the Houthis in Yemen and Shia militias in Iraq and Syria. And on the home front, the Iranian regime engages in significant human rights abuses to maintain its brutal stranglehold on the Iranian people.

House Foreign Affairs Committee Chairman Royce and Ranking Member Engel recently introduced H.R. 1698, the Iran Ballistic Missiles and International Sanctions Enforcement Act, which I was glad to cosponsor. This bill strategically increases targeted pressure on those responsible for furthering Iran's development of ballistic missiles without mandating sanctions on a sweeping range of activities that may or may not be indirectly related to the missile program. In the interest of preventing that which we all can agree is an unacceptable outcome – a nuclear-armed Iran – Congress must work in concert with the Administration to ensure that the nuclear agreement is fully implemented and strictly enforced. That is why it is so important for

H.R. 1698 to carefully tailor U.S. sanctions against Iran in such a way that ensures compliance with the JCPOA.

Ultimately, the United States cannot address Iran's destabilizing behavior alone. The United States has been the leader of an international coalition of countries that coalesced around the shared goal of preventing Iran's development of a nuclear weapon. The importance of international unity to address Iran's other malign actions cannot be understated. Unilateral U.S. sanctions hold limited leverage when the United States barely registers on Iran's radar of trading partners. Furthermore, we cannot effectively address this issue if Russia continues to undermine global efforts to reign in Tehran's provocative behavior by reportedly supplying Iran's ballistic missile program and thwarting action at the U.N. Security Council.

I look forward to hearing from our witnesses regarding how Congress can defuse the threats posed by the Iranian regime, and maintain support for a robust international coalition.